KRISTIN
LOUISE
DUNCOMBE

TRAILING
a memoir

This work is a memoir based on some of the experiences I lived over four and a half years in East Africa as the wife of a Médecins Sans Frontières doctor. Certain situations and characters have been condensed, blended or modified, for the sake of protecting identity or improving narrative flow. For more information see Author's Note at the back of the book.

Copyright © 2012 Kristin Louise Duncombe

Published in the United States by CreateSpace
All Rights Reserved.

ISBN-10: 1470159791
ISBN-13: 9781470159795

1. Trailing Spouses 2. Médecins Sans Frontières – Humanitarian Aid 3. Africa 4. Husbands and Wives 5. Trauma and Anxiety 6. Personal Identity

For my mother,
who taught me how to tell a story

PROLOGUE: NAIROBI, 1998

"I think a car is following us," my husband says suddenly, almost midnight on the way home from a party.

In Nairobi, this can mean only one of two things: Someone wants your car, or someone wants you.

"Drive faster!" I implore, although he's already floored the accelerator of our old Toyota.

We have turned down the road we live on, pitch black, except for moonlight coming through the jacaranda trees.

At the gate of our minimum-security compound my husband veers sharply into the driveway. He does not signal or slow down, so the car behind us shoots past. For a split second my heart rejoices.

It was all in my head.

Then, the sound of tires screeching as the driver slams on the brakes.

Oh God. It's happening.

Men pour into the road. There are four. No, five. Tall. Young. They have guns. Pistols. Kalashnikovs.

My husband puts the car in reverse, but loses control of the vehicle. We spin 180 degrees and end up with our back wheels in the ditch next to our driveway. The engine stalls.

The men are running toward us, and then they are there, guns pointed through our windows. They are well dressed, well groomed. One is wearing a lot of gold. A gold pocket watch. A heavy chain.

I am frozen in my seat when they yank open the doors and pull us from the car. It is rough and fast and I say, "I am very frightened," dropping down, as though I might play dead. One of our captors, the very thin one with a thick wedding band, pulls me up by the arm. He does not look at me but does not let go, pointing his gun at my head.

From other people's stories, I know what is supposed to follow: being taken on a joyride, then dumped. The gangsters will keep the car. If we are lucky I will not be raped, and if we are very lucky, we will make it out alive.

They shove us into the back of our vehicle. I am thigh to thigh with my husband, men on either side of us, their weapons trained on our heads. Two of the others jump into the front seat; the fifth runs back to the car they left up the road, engine running.

When the man in the driver's seat of our car tries to start the ignition, it doesn't work. He tries a few more times, and then he gets mad.

He shouts something in a language I don't recognize and they all get out of the car, pulling my husband after them. I am left alone in the back seat until my thin captor climbs in again and puts the gun back to my temple.

From where I sit all I can see of my husband is his torso. The men make a circle around him, pushing him back and forth, shouting "Start the car! Show us how to start the car!"

He tries to respond but they won't let him, hitting him in the back and legs with the butts of their guns. A sudden crack is the sound of metal hitting his skull. He drops to his knees, moaning.

I plead from the back seat. *Please don't kill him.*

And then, as though in slow motion, the headlights of another car illuminate the scene. As it nears, the driver stops abruptly and takes off in reverse at high speed, the lights disappearing as he rounds a corner. All that remains of our witness is the roar of his engine as he gets away, saving only himself, as one learns to do in Nairobi.

Yet it is enough to break the moment. As suddenly as they came upon us, our captors abandon us at the scene, our vehicle in the ditch, me alone in the back seat, my husband on the ground a few feet away.

They speed off shouting *Fuck you, muzungu!*

I fall out of the car, sobbing but so relieved, so incredibly grateful to be alive. My husband picks himself up off the ground. We clutch each other and run toward the gate. It opens with a gracious swing, the teenage boy who is meant to guard us cowering in the darkness, the padlock in his hand.

My husband wants to go back out for the car; I beg him to wait until daylight, just a few hours. Back in our house, we face each other in the dim of our small bedroom. His bruised head and knees are already swelling. We rock back and forth in each other's arms, holding each other so tightly it is painful.

I feel something fragile inside me - some painful recognition of the nearness of death and the gift of life – and I know right then that I want to have a child. I want to use my life to give life, to sustain it.

I cannot stop shaking, curled against my husband, whose breathing finally evens and I know he has fallen asleep. I have an image of my mother learning about my murder, as though it had actually turned out that way. The crickets are singing as they do in the early morning, but their song no longer makes sense. It is foreign to my ears, which are filled with a foggy noise, as though a terrible explosion has left me partially deaf.

NEW ORLEANS

How does a young American woman find herself being carjacked in Nairobi, Kenya?

To explain, I have to go back to Louisiana in the summer of 1995.

I went to New Orleans to build a career and put down some roots. Instead, I got married and followed my husband to East Africa.

My friends and family weren't surprised, given that I'd spent my childhood traveling, the daughter of a US Foreign Service officer. By the time I turned 18, I had lived in the United States, Cote d'Ivoire, Egypt, India, and Indonesia.

It was exhilarating to live such a cosmopolitan existence. But life as a "diplomatic brat" meant permanent enrollment in a social skills boot camp. You learned to make friends quickly and adjust just as fast to losing them. It led to a sense of feeling at home everywhere...and nowhere at all, for "home" was perpetually changing, oriented around Dad's career, and whichever end of the earth it required us to be in.

I arrived in Louisiana, barely 26 years old but relocating for the third time since my arrival back in the US eight years earlier. I'd been in New Orleans for all of a day when I met Tano, a handsome Argentinian seven years my senior.

Tano (an "argentismo" for *Italiano,* a nickname that referred to his Italian roots and dual Argentinian-Italian citizenship) was already a doctor – and, moreover, on the staff of *Médecins Sans Frontières,* the near-legendary community of health-care professionals. MSF had been created in 1971 by a small group of French physicians as a response to the humanitarian disaster following the secession of Biafra from the Republic of Nigeria. It believed that people everywhere, regardless of race, religion, or political affiliation, had the right to medical care, and that their need superseded respect for national borders. With its dedication and lack of concern for profit, comfort or even safety, MSF had speedily become, in the public imagination at least, something like a medical priesthood – part Red Cross, part Indiana Jones.

Compared to the misfits I normally attracted, Tano was the boyfriend of my dreams – professional, presentable, full of purpose - and so *foreign,* the perfect companion for someone who, though I could pass as just another young American, felt alien in my own country: American by passport, but not *really.*

In spite of his appeal, though, I was reluctant to get involved. It may have seemed as though I were playing hard to get, but the truth was that I had come to New Orleans weary of men, bruised by a long string of complicated and failed liaisons. In hindsight I could see how my rootlessness fed these failures - I got involved too quickly. A sense of urgency permeated my relationships, and often overshadowed both common sense and good judgment. This had been problematic for me as a teenager and young woman, and I had arrived in Louisiana determined to stay clear of men and focus on what I hoped would be the launch of my career in clinical social work.

But Tano was irresistible. His melodic accent turned me into *Kreeestin* - the 'r' rolling off his tongue - and I basked in being the love object on which he lavished his charming, linguistically-flawed invitations - to *planify a dee-ner* and spend some *times* together. He was typically Argentinian, I would come to learn. Fiercely political, he believed in the possibility of social revolution, yet he was also calm, relaxed, always ready to prepare *mate* – a South American tea, served in a small gourd and sipped from a silver *bombilla* - and sit around the table discussing, or playing the guitar and singing ballads.

Tano had graduated from medical school in Argentina the same year I returned to the United States for college. When I was doing my undergraduate work at Mount Holyoke in Massachusetts, Tano was already in Thailand and then Uganda, working as a doctor in sprawling refugee camps. When I moved out to Seattle to teach sex education to incarcerated teenagers and street kids, Tano was running slum clinics in Guatemala and community health projects in the Brazilian jungle. I liked to think of our separate paths as having been on a trajectory, propelling us towards New Orleans and each other. I should have known that trajectories, once having intersected, immediately start to diverge, but geometry wasn't required knowledge for a therapist.

We rented a mint-green cottage on a quiet street in Uptown New Orleans. Magnolias lined the path leading to our house, dropping their velvet flowers into the sleepy cemetery next door. The grass around the tombstones was cut weekly and the fresh, wet smell lingered in the air for days after, reminding me of childhood visits to my grandparents.

Over the next eighteen months we went to school and I also went to work, doing my clinical training as a therapist in a substance-abuse treatment center. The practicum was hands-on, rigorous, and I hoped to be hired after graduation. I daydreamed about settling down with Tano, me working as a therapist, he as a doctor...

"But my work is with people in *poor* countries," he insisted one night over dinner. "You *know* that. When I'm done with school, I'll go back to MSF."

He *had* told me that – repeatedly. I knew his political commitment to humanitarian medicine, a decision he'd made as a student in the 1980s when Argentina was controlled by a military dictatorship installed by the CIA. Thousands of people were tortured and murdered. Across South and Central America, poverty spread, disease and suffering rampant in the *villas miseria*. He'd heard of MSF, and a week after getting his medical degree, left for Europe to join them. He only bought a one-way ticket. Already, he knew his life's work.

With our joint graduation fast approaching, Tano began to receive emails from MSF, proposing missions in places that sounded dauntingly remote and hostile: Afghanistan, Somalia, Iran.

"Marry me," Tano urged. "Come with me to the field."

"But I don't want to live in a war zone."

"You won't have to. If we're married, MSF will only offer me missions in places that are suitable for a spouse."

"But what about *my* career?"

"You'll find work, too. The most important thing is that we stay together."

I just stared at him, remembering all the places my father's career had carted me off to over the years. I knew firsthand how to relocate because of someone else's obligations; that I'd never seen my mother contest that system certainly contributed to how normal it felt to embark on that journey again. Deep down it actually felt like a *relief* to follow Tano, far easier than having to launch myself professionally, earn a living, and take full responsibility for creating an adult life.

Still, some part of me already craved geographic stability, to have *roots*. And I certainly didn't want my "career" to be the piecing together of odd jobs, as I'd seen so many Foreign Service wives do. So I argued.

"Why can't you take a job with MSF New York?" Although the headquarters was in Paris, MSF had base operations in many capitals, not just in medical danger zones.

The fact that we had this conversation about three thousand times was a testament not just to Tano's patience, but also to his consistency, as from day one he never, ever deviated from his position:

"The United States government is behind military dictatorships that have killed *hundreds of thousands* of innocent people around the world. I'd be selling my soul to become a part of the US system."

Sometimes when Tano spoke like this, I felt as if I was attending a political meeting (with an audience of only one). But his conviction was so complete…and I was so in love with him….

"Would you *really* leave me behind if I wouldn't go where MSF sent you?" I grappled with him again one evening.

A long silence passed. He didn't break eye contact but he didn't answer either, and I finally stormed away from the table, acting angry but feeling vulnerable.

In our bedroom, a heap of clothing lay on the floor, discarded hastily late one night when the only urgency was to cling to each other under the covers.

If I didn't go along with his plans, I'd lose him.

I picked up a sweater and folded it, an overwhelming sense of loss welling inside me: loss of my budding professional identity, loss of Tano, loss of control. I dropped the sweater back on the heap and sat down on the floor, burying my face in my hands. All I could think of suddenly were the tomato seedlings we had grown in half of an empty milk carton. Tano had gotten the seeds right out of a fresh tomato. *How did he know these things?* Now they were little plants, cheerfully green in our kitchen window, where the morning sun poured in as we kissed goodbye over half drunk cups of coffee.

I went to bed on my own that night, but instead of sleeping I tossed and turned, replaying Tano's words: *The most important thing is that we stay together.*

I got up, finally, to pee, but as I padded down the hallway I could hear music coming from the living room.

Tano was sitting on the sofa, curled over his guitar and singing quietly. I watched for a moment and then went to him.

"*Mi amor*," he whispered, looking up. "You're still awake."

"I can't sleep."

"Come sit." He patted the sofa and returned to his song, this time pausing between every line to translate the words:

Dale alegría, alegría a mi corazón,
Give joy to my heart,
Es lo único que te pido, al menos hoy,
It's all I ask, at least for today,
Dale alegría, alegría a mi corazón,
Give joy to my heart
Y que se enciendan las luces de este amor
And turn on the lights of this love
Y ya verás cómo se transforma el aire del lugar,
And you will see how the air of this place is transformed
Y ya verás que no necesitaremos nada más.
And you will see - we won't need anything else.

Years later I would recognize this as the turning point: the moment where an internal switch got flipped, and I suppressed my instincts, forgetting, really, that I still even had a choice in the matter. Of the two of us, *he* was the imperative one, I believed – established already as a *doctor*, whereas I was still in formation, with some dreams, maybe, but completely unfinished as a person.

A career as a psychotherapist wasn't obligatory, I rationalized. *I could do lots of different things for work. And being Tano's wife would provide another sense of identity and purpose.*

I took the guitar from his hands. Then I turned off the lights, the moonlight-soaked night coming in through the window. Slipping out of my clothes, I walked towards him, stealthy as an Indian moving in a forest of dry leaves. In that moment I still knew what I was doing.

He slid down on the sofa to meet me as I straddled him, running my hands through his hair and guiding his mouth to mine.

"What are you doing to me?" His breath tingled over my lips.

"Relax," I whispered. "There's something I want to give you."

A few months later we were married, in a do-it-ourselves ceremony at the Parkview Guesthouse on the edge of Audubon Park in uptown New Orleans. The Parkview was an elegant but neglected old mansion, and its dilapidated condition would strike me later as a prophecy, but the weekend of our wedding we barely had time to notice the threadbare carpet and the peeling wallpaper. We were too busy cooking and cleaning and decorating alongside our out of town guests who were staying in the Guesthouse.

My parents, who were absolutely thrilled about my engagement, drove down from Washington, DC where they had recently retired. Composed, intellectual people, they had worried about my "prospects" after a rebellious, oppositional adolescence: going out with "greasers," coming home from parties drunk or stoned, well past curfew. Although I had always continued to do well in school, I moved into young adulthood in a similar fashion, making spotty decisions when it came to men.

But now I was finally settling down – and with a doctor! They were as relieved for me as they were impressed by him.

"So *smart*," my mother said.

"A good man," my father agreed. "He'd have no trouble finding work at the NIH."

The National Institute of Health was based in Bethesda, Maryland, right near where my parents now lived. This was only the first of a string of references to the possibility of Tano working there "after" MSF. Cautiously I dropped hints that Tano "really felt he could do more in the developing world" or "had a very clear idea of the best thing for his career." But they didn't read between the lines, and I couldn't quite find the words to explain that he did not share their attachment to the American way, and that I was about to recreate the model of life they'd raised me in.

The day of the ceremony we barely had time to go home to shower and slip into our wedding clothes – Tano had bought a suit for the occasion and I a backless black velvet ball gown. When we pulled back up at the Guesthouse, all our family members and a crowd of friends from the Schools of Public Health and Social Work were waiting outside. They applauded as we walked up the path, into the house and to the judge, who was waiting for us in the center of the room. I felt like a movie star being awarded an Oscar.

A few weeks later, we both received our leather bound diplomas. Tano advised MSF offices around Europe that he was ready to return to work, and I began perusing the job pages of the *Times Picayune*, figuring that we'd have *some* time before he was offered a mission.

Yet barely a day after sending off his emails he was barraged with calls. MSF-France, MSF-Holland, MSF-Spain and MSF-Switzerland all proposed missions. But all were in places either too dangerous, too remote, or in some other way impossible for a "non-essential" spouse.

Non-essential. The term burned in my ears.

"I thought you said if we got married MSF would only propose missions that I could go to as well."

"They need doctors," he replied simply.

In the middle of all of this, I received a phone call from Lillian, the mother of an old high school friend I'd known in New Delhi, but now divorced from her Foreign Service husband. We met for lunch the following day. Her appearance shocked me. She looked drained, used up.

"It was never easy to follow him," she said, as we sat before steaming bowls of Gumbo at a French Quarter restaurant. "If you find the trailing life isn't for you, I hope you have the good sense to get out early and not suffer for thirty years as I did."

The trailing life? She made it sound like being a U-Haul. But looking back, I could remember my friend confiding to me her mother's bouts of depression and the drinking binges – though always in deepest secrecy: a Foreign Service family could be recalled to Washington if it became known there were "problems at home."

I tried to sound optimistic. "Oh, I'm not worried. I grew up with it, I'm prepared."

Lillian patted my hand. "You'll see," she said. "Once you leave the States and start moving around, everything changes."

At home, the pressure mounted. MSF-Switzerland lobbied Tano for weeks to accept a mission in the central African country of Burundi, which had been plunged in civil war since 1993. The situation in Burundi paralleled the genocide that had occurred in neighboring Rwanda in 1994, where hundreds of thousands of Tutsis had been massacred by the Hutus. It was a year's assignment, but when Tano refused because he couldn't bring me along, MSF offered to cut the contract to six months. He still declined, and inwardly I was torn between the guilt that thousands of Tutsis desperately needed a doctor, and were denied one because of me, and the utter relief of not having to live in a war zone.

In the shower one morning, I was ruefully reflecting on Lillian's warning, no longer able to suppress a growing sense of unease about this life I'd married into. Suddenly Tano burst into the bathroom.

"We've found a solution!"

MSF-France had called from Paris. Their mission in Nairobi, Kenya's capital, that served as the hub for foreign development and humanitarian projects all over Eastern, Central and Southern Africa, needed a *Med-Co* – Medical Coordinator. Tano would oversee all their interventions: a clinic in the slums of Nairobi, an HIV/AIDS and tuberculosis treatment project in a western town on Lake Victoria, and all other epidemics or crises as they occurred. And *anyone* could go to Nairobi - even a non-essential wife.

One week later, we touched down at Jomo Kenyatta International Airport. It was after 10 PM as we went through immigration. The officer in the booth was stern as he examined our passports.

"Tourism?" he asked.

"Work," Tano replied. "I am a doctor with Médecins Sans Frontières."

"Her?" He glanced speculatively at me.

"She is my wife."

I smiled in a way I hoped look appropriately serene, fighting off the sense of regression I was privately feeling. The officer stamped our visas, and from the belly of the Nairobi airport we came through the doors to the arrival lounge. A crowd was piled up on the other side of a wooden barrier: solemn drivers in safari suits holding signs with hotel logos to the right, Kenyan families exclaiming joyful hellos to the left.

We scanned the crowd. A thin, thirty-something white man with a head of curly blonde hair held up a sign with the MSF logo. I approached him, extending my hand in greeting, but he gave me a perfunctory *bise,* the kiss on both cheeks used by the French to say hello and goodbye. He bestowed the same on Tano and said, in French, "I am Guillaume. Welcome to Nairobi."

KENYA

I leaned into the back seat of the white Toyota Corolla as we roared erratically down the Mombasa highway, Guillaume swerving around the numerous pot holes. Later I discovered that giraffes and zebras grazed in the open country through which we drove, but that evening the blackness of the night was impenetrable.

Guillaume was the Head of Mission, and had already been in Nairobi for a year. He and Tano launched straight into a discussion about MSF's operations in Kenya. They spoke French, but though I understood almost everything – four years as a child in francophone West Africa had made me quite proficient - I felt rusty and too self conscious to speak.

As well, I was re-experiencing Africa, although at first glance I did not see any of the signs that had marked my childhood in the tropics: palm trees, bamboo huts, stacks of dried fish being sold on the roadside by women dressed in traditional clothes.

Here, we drove through long, empty stretches, the monotony broken only by the occasional billboard or clumps of apartment buildings behind barbed wire fences, lights off. Darkness. As we entered downtown Nairobi, concrete structures, grayed and ramshackle, rose up in silent greeting, as though keeping watch along the broad, barren avenues.

Abruptly Guillaume switched to English, calling to me over his shoulder.

"You are *americaine?*"

"Yes, from Washington DC."

"You are aware of what your country is doing in Kisangani right now?" His accent was almost exaggeratedly French, his *r*'s throaty, his *th*'s sounding like *z*'s, and it took a moment to understand his words. But the hostility in his voice was clear from the start.

"I, uh...no," I stuttered nervously, racking my brains for anything I could remember about Kisangani. He saved me by answering his own question.

"Your government got their friend Kabila in office, and US business has already moved in. Diamonds." His voice was thick with combativeness. "The Americans get richer while the Congolese starve."

How naïve was I, thinking that we'd chat about the best markets for buying fabric and where to shop for bread – all the conversational pleasantries that my mother had relied on when we were posted to a new country. Tuning out the accusation, I stared out the window. Women clad in scanty, garish outfits hawked themselves on dim street corners, and groups of shabbily dressed men looked on. The scene looked as if it had been dumped there, taking root by accident in the middle of the savanna.

We drove along in silence for a few more minutes and then Guillaume said, *"Alors le voici, chez vous."*

The car swung off the road, its lights illuminating a high metal gate. He slammed his hand down twice, hard, on the horn, and with a squeal of unoiled hinges, it began laboriously to swing inwards.

The next day, I explored our new home. "Chez nous" was an apartment on Rhapta Road, in a neighborhood called Westlands. By Kenyan standards, it was middle-class, but still, ragged kids sniffing glue loitered nearby on its street corners and garbage piled up on the roadside. We were the sole *muzungus* – white people - in the apartment building, which was otherwise filled with *muindis* - Kenyan Indians. The only black Africans were the ones who worked there: cleaning ladies, babysitters, and the guards, young men barely out of adolescence.

Across the street was the MSF office, a functional brick duplex, standing in the midst of a garden, bursting with flowering bushes around which little yellow birds flittered. The front door was shrouded in a halo of flaming pink bougainvillea, and a tree in the yard scattered tiny white blossoms all over the grass, its branches providing shade for the cars - identical white Toyota Corollas all in a row.

As if to scorn the natural calm and tranquility of its surroundings, the MSF office boiled over with activity. Phones rang ceaselessly, Kenyan secretaries snatching them up. The Kenyan guards and drivers were kept just as busy clanging the gate open and shut to accommodate the comings and goings of the expatriate staff: doctors on their way to Sudan, nurses just back from Rwanda, logisticians going to Congo, plus the team that dealt with the innumerable health problems of Kenya itself.

Tano crossed the street early every morning and returned most evenings around 9:00 to fetch me so that we could join the team at whichever MSF house would host that evening's *apero* - the French before-dinner drink. I knew Tano wanted me to feel included. And, to be fair, his colleagues did make an effort to communicate with me.

But it was hard to fit in. As the scotch or wine circulated, the polemic would unfurl. Most of the MSFers had witnessed terrible genocides - Biafra, Salvador, Rwanda, Bosnia. And like Guillaume, many didn't miss a chance to assert their anti-Americanism, and to point out that my country had played a prominent role in almost all these horrific crimes against humanity.

At first I was fascinated. Only someone who read the NEW YORK TIMES every day from front page to back could have accumulated so much information. But I quickly got tired - of being confronted about US foreign policy, as though I were guilty by association, and then by the omnipresence of the team, and what seemed to be its sole subject of conversation: the past, present, and future of MSF.

A few times I tried to change the topic with one of the friendlier members of the team, Fabienne, the doctor in charge of the slum clinic, who was the ultimate *femme extraordinaire*. Hardcore MSF, effortlessly stylish *and* a gourmet chef.

"Mmmmm," I sniffed over her shoulder one evening, as she casually whipped up a *coq au vin* with braised potatoes. "Where did you learn to cook like that? You should have your own restaurant."

She shrugged in an offhand French way and didn't answer, smoothing over the awkward moment by pouring each of us another glass of wine. The message was clear. In the midst of so much poverty and suffering, this was not an appropriate question. I felt as if I'd asked a nun where she had her nails done.

Inevitably, the boozy aspect of the teams' gatherings reminded me of my diplomatic childhood. Alcohol had flowed just as copiously at Embassy parties, and even we kids were aware that a lot more went on behind the scenes than was ever acknowledged by our parents. But Kenya added another ingredient to the mix. Marijuana was powerful, plentiful and cheap. Joints circulated freely at the MSF soirées, and while of course not everyone smoked, those who cared to never went without.

During those first weeks in Nairobi, I took the joints as peace pipes – something I could share with the team, no matter how intimidated I felt. But there was a downside. Just a few puffs of the powerful weed and I became silly, reckless, unable any longer to suppress my frustration at this communal life.

"I heard your snores last night," I blurted to Guillaume one evening. *Apero* the evening before had taken place at our apartment, and he'd passed out. We left him on the sofa to sleep it off.

"Imagine poor me," Fabienne said, not missing a beat, "I once had to share a tent with him in Kigali. Most people didn't sleep because of the gunfire. Me, it was because of Guillaume."

Everyone laughed, and the conversation switched back to those times they'd shared in Rwanda.

Occasionally, the social diet of MSF was varied by guests from some other expat group. The UN guy who supplied the pot sometimes arrived with one or even two teenage "girlfriends" - prostitutes he'd picked up for the night.

"Those girls are practically *children*," I said one evening. We had been drinking and smoking and the accusation slipped out.

"They're old enough." Sober, he might have denied that he'd paid them – or told me it was none of my business. But the booze and the weed brought the barriers down. "And I genuinely like them." He regarded the girls with the bleary expression of drunks everywhere. "When a man and a woman feel attraction for one another, it's...well, love."

I looked at the giggling, half-stoned adolescents in their gaudy, revealing clothes. How could he delude himself that love was involved in this transaction? Or that these girls were even attracted to him – pudgy, bald and aging. This was pure commerce. A night with a *muzungu* could help a Kenyan girl support her family for a month or more. Here was the relationship between Africa and the developed world, in sordid microcosm.

If I'd thought life as an MSF wife would replicate the cushioned lifestyle of my childhood in the Foreign Service, I was quickly shown otherwise. Our apartment was austere, furnished with battered discards. Even if someone had cared to think about furnishings, they would hardly have had time between medical crises. Hence the sagging rattan couches and armchairs with their frayed, faded cushions; the threadbare towels and sheets, the battered aluminum pots and mismatched knives and forks.

Nor, unlike the US Foreign Service, did MSF offer much in the way of logistical support to spouses. Our apartment had no telephone, nor did I have regular access to a car or driver.

Fortunately, I could use the phone at Tano's office, and it was only ten minutes' walk to the center of Westlands, a roundabout where restaurants, shops and even a French bakery sprouted. I got used to weaving through the traffic, and dodging street vendors, hustlers and beggars. A small, Indian-owned book shop stocked novels and self-help books imported from the UK. I often took my purchases and sat in the bakery for hours, reading, drinking cappuccinos topped with big swirls of whipped cream, while guiltily keeping my eyes on the window lest one of the hardworking MSFers pass by and see me in my idle indulgence.

Off the Roundabout was a branch of *Uchumi*, the local grocery store chain. Like any Western style grocery, it offered dairy and fresh produce, as well as aisles of canned goods, many of which were imported from the UK and India. There I bought staple items like rice and flour, but all of our fresh food came from the outdoor market across the street. The market was an herbivore's dream, stall after stall heaped with succulent fruit and colorful vegetables. I went to market almost every day and bought plump bananas bursting out of their skins, fragrant passion fruits, eggplants, peppers, papaya...

Best of all was the *mitumba* –the second hand clothing stalls. Stylish clothes – factory rejects, surplus stock, and Goodwill donations sent over in barrels from Europe and America - hung for sale on the side of the road. After stocking up on fruits and vegetables, one could find name-brand and designer items...at one 500th of the price for which they'd be sold in the West. Low prices confounded my Western ideas of class; it always struck me to see, of two *mamas* selling tomatoes in the vegetable market, one sporting a jersey with the logo of the men's lacrosse team from some obscure private school in the USA, the other a discarded *Dolce e Gabbana* t-shirt.

Digging for an attractive "new" article at the *mitumba* brought to the surface some of the conflicting emotions I discovered those first weeks back on African soil. Rejects from the West were treasures to those of us in Africa, whether *muzungu, muindi* or black. And although the vendors adjusted prices according to the skin color of their customer, everyone could afford to shop at the clothing stalls. I didn't mind paying the "*muzungu* price" for clothes or food. It felt fair, given the poverty around us.

But our own "poverty" became an issue when Tano confronted me about the amount I was spending at the *mitumba* and the French Bakery. Although prices were reasonable by any Western standard, such "luxuries" strained the modest per diem allocated from MSF's budget.

Had I been more forthcoming, I might have explained to Tano that I hung out in Westlands to avoid a mounting panic. Drinking coffee, reading, and buying fashionable cast-offs was an attempt to forget the career I was not pursuing and an effort to recreate the pampered position of the diplomatic child. Mostly, though, it was something to *do*, an attempt to quell the loneliness that had surged inside me. Because though I could shop for clothes with the Africans, I couldn't stop being a *muzungu* to them: an icon of colonial plunder, western decadence, an *opportunity*, to be taken advantage of. Yet in the eyes of the *muzungus* who now comprised "my" community – the MSFers – I was just as much an alien – *l'américaine*, who fell on the wrong side of the foreign aid divide. Who could blame them for seeing me that way, when rarely (if ever?) did I come up with anything very useful when it came to their savvy intellectual discussions.

But God, how I *longed* to fit in with them; to share their steely dedication. Early on, part of me even believed that simply being married to Tano would be the catalyst for my transformation, that his tireless work ethic would replace my bumbling insecurity and turn me into someone who could also be part of the team. But I couldn't very well head for the frontlines of disease and disaster when I had never seen a corpse, let alone an epidemic, and could barely bandage a cut finger without feeling faint.

Were Tano the one recounting our first months in Kenya, I would certainly be featured as the schizophrenic crazy: charming, presentable, and even kowtowing in the presence of the team, keen to demonstrate my adoration of *their* medical coordinator, my husband. Yet the minute we were alone (the fact that we were rarely alone is probably what saved us in those early months) I would turn on him, unleashing all of my frustration, blaming him for my decision to follow him to Nairobi.

In the midst of my personal plight, a jolting sense of the real Africa was provided by Mama Florence, the MSF housekeeper who visited our apartment every morning. A jovial, God-fearing woman whose matronly breasts disappeared into her plump waist, she kept up a constant stream of chatter - in broken English, mixed with Kiswahili and her native Kikuyu, the language of the largest tribe in Kenya.

"I am widow," she said one day as we sat together in the kitchen. She was preparing *ugali* – a maize-based porridge – and *sukuma*, a kind of kale that grew abundantly in Kenya. The most popular dish was *sukuma wiki* - literally 'push the week' – on which even the poorest family could survive for days.

"My husband was cursed dead by an evildoer."

"*Cursed?*"

"He was not a smart man. He had one wife, but he wanted more. So he took a co-wife for me. But she could not give him *toto*." Toto was Kiswahili for child.

"She feel humiliated because I produced many *toto*," Mama Florence went on. "So she cursed him. He died of a chicken bone in the throat."

I had traveled all the way from New Orleans to be confronted by voodoo, I thought. Yet I wasn't really surprised. The forty year old "houseboy" who cooked and cleaned for my family in Cote d'Ivoire when I was a child had periodically hung lizards by their tails in the window of our kitchen.

This had always made my mother nervous. "Witchcraft," she'd say. "Maybe he's trying to jinx us."

Then, as now, I half-believed. So odd as some of her stories were, I couldn't discard Mama Florence's accounts. And because I had no idea how to just start a life out of thin air, I spoke freely of my desire to work.

Deep down I hoped that she would cast a spell on my behalf.

Before I left New Orleans, a professor at the School of Public Health told me I would have no trouble finding work in East Africa. "Contact USAID," he said. "They're everywhere. And they have a *huge* budget for consultants."

USAID – the US Agency for International Development – was indeed huge. And its regional headquarters was in Nairobi, in a large, modern and well-guarded complex which had been pointed out to me on my earliest orienting drive around the city.

It was through USAID that the American government channeled aid to countries like Kenya. But while its stated aim was "to extend assistance to countries recovering from disaster, trying to escape poverty, and engage...in democratic reforms," Tano and his colleagues spoke of it as an imperialistic octopus with tentacles all over the developing world, existing largely to provide handsome salaries and lavish lifestyles to American bureaucrats.

Rather than potentially compromise my reputation by selling out to USAID, I hadn't contacted them. Instead, Tano located a list of international non-governmental organizations and local charities working in Kenya, all more or less untainted by the corrupting Yankee dollar. It had more than sixty addresses and phone numbers on it.

So one morning when he was out of town I went over to MSF and closed myself in his office. One wall was filled with a big map of Kenya and another by an even bigger map of Nairobi. Both had little pins and pieces of paper with notes stuck on them stating the diseases in that district, and the contact person at the Ministry of Health there. Surely in this mass of impoverished people, there was an organization that could use me for *something*.

But an hour later, I was totally discouraged. I had called the first ten numbers, repeatedly, and couldn't get through to any of them... although it became worse when I did get through.

"I am a social worker and I'm looking for work," I would say.

"You're a special *what*?"

"SOCIAL worker," I would enunciate. "SOCIAL."

"*Special worker*? Special, *how*?"

I finally was able to leave messages at several local charities.

Encouraged, I called the United Nations in Nairobi - a lolling complex that looked like an elite country club.

The receptionist answered immediately and began impatiently rattling off names.

"Do you want UNDP? UNHCR? WFP? HABITAT? UNICEF?"

Tongue-tied, I hung up on her. Of all those acronyms UNICEF was the only one that I recognized, so I pushed the redial button on the phone.

"UNICEF, please," I said, making a gruff voice with what I hoped sounded like a British accent, so that she would not recognize that it was me again.

I was connected to a woman who sounded Japanese. She asked me the question I would become loath to answer: *What* did I do?

Well, what *did* I do? What skill could I offer these people, who already had access to any expert they required? Serious professionals, I had recently realized, were able to clarify *what* they were capable of doing. I told her I'd get back to her, grateful that I had not given my name.

After mulling it over for a few days, I decided it would be more effective to seek work in person. Armed with my resumé and Mama Florence's encouragement, I headed to the *matatu* stand at the Westlands roundabout.

Matatus were minivans, a type of public transport that Kenyans relied on. More than a dozen people could be jammed in, along with shopping bags, sheaves of *sukuma,* bulging bags of produce, and the occasional chicken. *Matatus* were notorious for their overcrowding and reckless speeding. Accidents were frequent.

When the first *matatu*, spray-painted with flashy images came barreling toward me, loud music blaring from its windows, I almost bolted. But the young man hanging out the side door was smiling.

"Hey *muzungu* - you want to ride?"

"Yes, please!"

I tried to sound enthusiastic. And it seemed fortuitous that the cassette they had playing was an old Alpha Blondy album; reminiscent of my days growing up in the Cote d'Ivoire, from where the popular singer hailed.

As I climbed in, fifteen pairs of eyes stared at me, some solemn, some with great amusement. I squeezed in between two large women with big bundles on their laps. The reggae rhythm was in perfect sync with the *matatu's* speeding wheels. Several passengers sang along as we sped towards town: *Cause I know now, that life ain't no dice... Yes I know now, that life is a sacrifice...*

Suddenly the woman next to me turned and said, "Excuse me, Madam. Can you donate money for my nephew's school fees?"

"I...I don't have any money to donate," I stuttered.

"Please madam. *Kitu kidogo*. Something small."

The man next to her chimed in. "We need you to sponsor us."

My feelings of ridiculousness were compounded when, tumbling off the *matatu* in downtown Nairobi, I dropped my folder of resumés into a puddle of muddy water. Frustrated and disheveled, I moved forward with the crowd, avoiding the cries of the beggars, and averting my eyes from their shocking physical deformities. Clearly one didn't see many *muzungus* moving around here on foot: children stared and Indian men in their vehicles honked and waved as I attempted to read my map, an endeavor I finally abandoned when a band of street kids surrounded me, pulling at my carefully chosen "professional" outfit, their hands and glue bottles grimy with the filth of Nairobi's streets.

I need donation, muzungu, they implored with a forlorn look in their eyes. *Sponsor me.*

Donate....sponsor.... The language of the aid culture adapted smoothly to simple pan-handling. This was the Africa that sprang from the developed world.

I got on the next *matatu* that came by and fled back to the safety of Westlands.

Before long, Tano began spending long stretches at the hospital in Nyanza province.

"There are no drugs in the pharmacy," he said one evening as we sat side by side on the balcony, sharing a beer. He was just home after his third trip in two months. "No running water. No way to get rid of garbage. Year after year the hospital waste – and that includes syringes and body parts - have been dumped in the courtyard. It's hardened into an actual floor."

He ran his finger absent-mindedly up and down my arm as he divulged the horror movie that was his work. And though I frequently accused him of being "unsupportive" and too busy to "share" with me, I only half listened, distracted by my intolerable jealousy of Tano's *access* to this lurid world. He had a life that used him up, while I sat around, *useless*, plunging further every day into an existential crisis: What was the point of *my* life?

"The hospital has no electricity either," he went on. "None of the machines are working – not even the refrigeration system of the morgue. We found a big pile of dead bodies there, rotting away, half-covered by a filthy plastic sheet. There are new bodies coming in every day and they get thrown onto the pile until the family pays the hospital fees and recovers them. In most cases, a family can't scrape up enough money to cover the hospital expenses, because they also have to raise money for the funeral."

Can you sponsor me, madam?

I imagined what it would be like to be one of those people — not the dead, their mortality spared them this putrid indignity — but the living, left behind to face life under these terrible conditions. Did the policy makers who controlled the foreign aid purse strings ever see these places?

Not that I bothered to ask. I had already sunk too deep into glum reticence, the negative mantra that had become my near constant companion drumming in my ears: *It's his fault that my career is going nowhere.*

"So as the pile of bodies grows," Tano continued, "the stench also grows. Just in the time I was there, the odor of rotting human flesh grew stronger and the wind carried this unbearable smell throughout the town. The police finally took action and buried all the bodies. They had to get a special 'emergency decree' to do it."

The happy cries of the *muindi* children playing in the courtyard below went suddenly forlorn as their mothers ordered them inside for dinner. Every evening there was a certain moment between dusk and night - marked by the guards' greetings to each other, up and down Rhapta Road - that served as a cue to go inside for the evening.

And then, silence.

Tano leaned over to embrace me. "Let's go to bed," he whispered, his fingers now entangled in my hair.

The last thing I wanted to do at that moment was make love. But instead of brushing away his advances, I went along with him, attempting to give the appearance of a woman who would at least be fulfilled in the bedroom. Who was I trying harder to deceive – Tano or myself? Because while I moaned and sighed at all the right moments, just beneath the surface my resentment and unhappiness festered like an abscess.

A few days later, Tano left for Nyanza again. On my first day alone, I headed for the French Bakery, hoping that a cinnamon swirl would ward off my gloom. But as I stepped out onto Rhapta Road, I bumped into Mama Florence.

"You have message from MSF telephone, Madam." She handed me a scrap of paper. On it was written:

SPECIAL WORKER NEEDED
PLEASE SEE SISTER GLADYS AT TEENAGE CLINIC.
KENYATTA HOSPITAL.

Kenyatta Hospital was the largest public hospital in Kenya. I could have kissed her.

Work!

I debated trying to *matatu* my way over to Kenyatta, but at the last minute headed to the taxi stand at the Westlands Roundabout instead. There was only one taxi parked there when I arrived. The fender hung off the back end of the car, one side was completely concave from what must have been a violent impact, and I could see through the window that the coils of the back seat were sticking out like the springs of a jack in the box.

"Where you go, Madam?" said the driver, a big man with small Rastafarian braids and CIA style sunglasses.

I told him. He grinned.

"No problem. I give you good discount."

He got out of the driver's seat with a crowbar in his hand, and I jumped backwards, prepared to run. But he just used it to pry the back door open. I hesitated for a moment and then allowed him to seal me into the backseat. A few minutes later we were puttering down the road.

At first I avoided his attempts at conversation, preferring that he concentrate on driving, but when it became clear that his car couldn't move any faster than twenty miles an hour, I lightened up.

"What did you say your name was?"

"Charles, Madam. I am from Kisumu."

Kisumu was the capital of Nyanza province, where MSF was conducting the HIV/TB intervention.

"I come to Nairobi to find wife," he offered conversationally. "In Kisumu there is no more chance. All ladies have the bad blood. *Ukimwi.*"

AIDS.

As we spoke, the taxi, which had barely skirted downtown Nairobi, turned right up a long hill, grinding in its lowest gear to wheeze up the incline. At the top, the streets became increasingly potholed and muddy. Garbage was strewn everywhere, cut by meandering paths where feet had stamped it down. This was a Nairobi I hadn't yet seen. Fewer beggars, no Indians – just Africans, getting on with their lives. Children in dirty tattered clothing played with a ball made of plastic bags, three women in a row braided each other's hair, vendors sold grilled ears of fresh corn.

Charles slowed down and the car shuddered to a halt. "This is Kenyatta Hospital."

A large concrete structure loomed ahead. The children abandoned their ball and swarmed around me.

"Give me one shilling, *muzungu*!"

Not so different then after all.

The children at my heels, I charged down the path towards the hospital, reassured that I was going in the right direction as the number of men in white doctors coats mixed increasingly in with the crowd.

Inside the Hospital compound, the crowd thickened. Two guards, ostensibly keeping watch, stood with their hands clasped in each others, deep in conversation. They looked amused when I approached.

"Excuse me, Sirs. Could you direct me to the Teenage Clinic?"

The elder of the two made a series of right and left hand gestures that sent me down various corridors, until I arrived at what could certainly be a counseling clinic. People clustered around the door of this unit, many in tears, some sobbing.

I took a deep breath and walked in.

A young man behind a desk stared at me. He seemed startled by my presence.

"Yes?"

"Sister Gladys called me for work."

He just stared blankly, so I repeated, "Sister Gladys?"

"You want to collect her?"

Assuming this was some linguistic euphemism, I nodded yes. He picked up a stack of paper and began to go through it, slowly, page by page.

"Sister Gladys, you say?"

"Yes."

"When did she die?"

"Die?" I was shocked. "I don't know. Is she dead?" I pulled the note Mama Florence had given me from my pocket and handed it to him.

He snorted. "This is not the Teenage Clinic, Madam. This is the morgue."

When I finally found Sister Gladys, a short, round woman with hundreds of tiny braids cascading down her back, I refrained from telling her that ten minutes earlier I had been looking for her dead body. It felt like a bad omen.

The Teenage Clinic was chipper compared to the rest of Kenyatta that I'd seen. A fresh coat of paint covered the walls and a brand new TV/VCR stood at the front of the waiting room. Sitting before it were approximately thirty young women, watching a video that alternated Kiswahili and English. In it, a village girl came to Nairobi and got involved with a "Sugar Daddy" who promised to pay her school fees. Instead, he made her pregnant, and infected her with HIV.

The modern spiffiness of the unit was explained by the grant money that funded the clinic, channeled through an NGO that received its funding from USAID. The purpose of the Teenage Clinic was to provide reproductive health services and counseling to teenagers, as evidenced by the brightly colored posters with messages about *Ukimwi* and the notorious Sugar Daddy on the wall. I knew already from accounts from MSF's slum clinic that older men infected with the HIV virus sought young virgins as partners. This was but one of many folkloric "cures" for AIDS.

"These teenagers have problems," Sister Gladys said.

We stood at the reception area after she'd introduced me to the four other nurses – Sisters, as they were called in Kenya – and dug through the heap of loose papers that constituted the patients files.

"Many problems. They are poor. And there is much AIDS. Rape. Incest. Masturbation--"

"*Masturbation?*"

"Oh, yes. We have a very bad case."

She handed me the notes from sessions with a young man who had been to the clinic on three separate occasions...because he masturbated every day. The notes indicated that Sister Gladys had made earnest attempts to educate him against this habit. Her language belonged in a Victorian manual of sexual pathology, and I couldn't help but think back to my days teaching Sex Ed at Juvenile Detention in Seattle where we had *encouraged* masturbation as a safer alternative to intercourse.

"We are blessed to have a *muzungu* working with us," Sister Gladys said, cutting into my thoughts. "You will help us with your knowledge of counseling."

I suppressed my concerns – that I spoke no Kiswahili and that it was not at all clear to me how the Western concepts of psychotherapy that I'd studied would be relevant to working with hungry clients who lived in dangerous slums – and followed Sister Gladys to my "office," a broom closet just large enough for two wooden chairs.

I saw my first client that afternoon, a girl of thirteen who had been sexually assaulted the evening before. With her shaved head, I might have taken her for a boy, were she not wearing a simple cotton dress. A sweaty odor emanated from her skin, filling the tiny room as she began her account in broken English, her eyes fixed at some point just beyond my shoulder.

"To my shack, it be necessary to cross the garbage pile." Her face was hard and grim. "I see the man has following me and so I run."

Suddenly the girl broke from English to Kiswahili, her voice rising as tears ran down her cheeks. She gripped the plastic cover of her notebook so hard the lines of her knuckles appeared as pinkish white as my own.

I could only understand a fraction of what she was saying, but between the words and her gestures, I knew: *this* was when he had jumped her, *this* was when he held her down, *this* was when he forced her legs open and penetrated her.

"I say no!" she sobbed. "I say no but he don't to listen."

Back in my apartment that evening, I lay face down on the bed, thinking about that poor girl at Kenyatta.

I say no.

My mind combed back through all the coursework I'd done on counseling techniques. But in the face of this trauma, the lack of any concrete intervention, such as medication to interrupt HIV infection or pregnancy, was distressing. I couldn't even offer her a shower.

The sound of Tano's key in the door brought me back to the present. Nightfall. Nairobi, Kenya.

Time for *apero* with the MSF team.

That evening the MSF team toasted me, and I basked in their astonishment that I had found a way "in" to this Kenyan hospital. Pleased also to show that not all Americans were greedy and capitalistic, I made sure they understood that I would be working as a *volunteer*. I decided not to share the news – not even with Tano (*lying about taxi fare wasn't really duplicitous, was it?*) - that, daunted by the prospect of getting there by other means, I'd struck a deal with Charles, the taxi driver. For 1000 shillings – roughly forty dollars at the time – he would take me back and forth to Kenyatta Hospital twice a week.

By the end of my second week of work, however, I had already begun to wonder if the expense was worth it. Sister Gladys' optimistic expectation of many English-speaking patients wasn't realized. There were long hours when I found myself conspicuously unoccupied, the only *muzungu* in the clinic - and the only person without something to do.

"You have to take charge," Tano advised when I told him how discouraged I felt. "There must be a hundred things that you could do in that clinic."

His words felt like a challenge. And I found my answer almost immediately in the clinic filing system. The "system," in fact, was no system at all – just a random stack of papers kept on the reception counter, freely rifled through by any patients who cared to search for their records.

Client confidentiality at the Kenyatta clinic seemed to be a *muzungu* concept, since I never saw a patient complain about the way private information was stored, nor did I ever witness someone digging through the pile just to read some juicy tidbit about someone else.

Still, with so much time on my hands, why not try and improve it?

I started by requesting file folders from Sister Gladys, who said she would ask Dr. Muthaiga, the hospital executive that liaised directly with the funding NGO and USAID. But when weeks had passed and none appeared, I went out and purchased some so that I could get to work alphabetizing the patient files.

As though proactivity spurred action, the English-speaking clientele began to emerge to fill all those fresh new folders with information. And as if my curiosity had willed him to me, one of my clients turned out to be the young masturbator. Our first session was a brief fifteen minutes – the time it took to assure him that it was normal at age 16 to, as he put it, "wank" - a vulgar Briticism transformed into something charming by his rich accent and the sincerely troubled expression on his face.

But when he came back two days later, I understood that the advice I gave in Seattle had to be tempered to the local beliefs. When he explained the counsel of the *muzungu* lady to his family and friends in the slum, they expressed horror. Everyone knew he would make himself infertile or that his penis would shrivel up and fall off if he kept up the sinful behavior.

I learned to go carefully, letting the clients explain their concerns, and what they thought I could do to help. Some of the most effective "techniques" were found in the well-tried adages we'd used freely at the substance abuse clinic in New Orleans. One was the serenity prayer, often said at the end of any Twelve Step meeting. Sister Gladys liked it so much that I printed it out for her and she taped it to the wall: *God grant me the serenity to accept the things I cannot change, courage to change the things I can, and the wisdom to know the difference.*

I also fell back on two of the most familiar of AA sayings that needed no cultural interpretation. *Take it easy* and *One day at a time.*

"Oh Madam!" exclaimed the seventeen year old girl I was working with one day. "You mean *pole pole!*"

Pole, pronounced *po-lay*, was Kiswahili for *slowly*, but was used colloquially to mean "take it easy."

This girl had been working as a prostitute since she was fifteen, and initially saw me as no more than a connection to the wealthy world of the *muzungus*.

"Find me a white man, Madam. Please."

I could, I thought ironically, my mind flashing to the UN worker and his "true love" theory.

"Why do you want a *muzungu*?"

"Because whites have much money." It was the answer I was expecting. But then she surprised me. "And only a *muzungu* can take the virus from my body."

More folklore.

"Do you think you're infected?"

She put her hands over her face and spoke through her fingers. "I fear."

We spent two more sessions discussing the issue. She had used condoms infrequently: many men refused. And she'd had more partners than she could count, except for the *muzungus*. Those numbered six.

"Do you want to get tested?" I pressed gently one day.

"Why find out?" she said glumly. "Medicines cost much money."

But by the end of our meeting she had decided to have her blood drawn. I would give her the results the following week.

On Tuesday when I got to work Sister Gladys was waiting for me.

"Good news!" she said, pushing the results into my hand. "Your young prostitute has tested negative!"

I couldn't wait to tell her, to work with her on her resolution to protect herself with condoms from then on.

But when her appointment time arrived, she wasn't waiting at the desk. I took someone in her place, and hurried through the session, hoping she was just late.

Morning turned to afternoon, and still she didn't show up. For weeks thereafter I looked out for her every time I stepped into the waiting room.

But I never saw her again.

One evening Tano surprised me by dropping a pamphlet in my lap.

"Read this," he said. "We could go camping there this weekend if you'd like."

The pamphlet was for Hell's Gate – a National Park in the Rift Valley, the fertile lake region stretching hundreds of kilometers north of Nairobi. Just two hours by road from Nairobi, the Park was near Lake Naivasha and one of the few reserves in Kenya not inhabited by predatory animals.

"How romantic. You, me and the team. In a tent."

"Not the team. Just us," he laughed, although I could see his eyes tense and I instantly regretted my comment. I had complained incessantly about the lack of alone-time since we'd touched down in Kenya, and the first time he made an overture I'd scoffed at it.

Saturday morning we were on our way, and quickly, like all traces of urban existence, the tension between us dropped away: the bush was right there, just beyond the city limits. As we drove through an immense valley dappled with rich greens and browns, cool moisture hanging in the air, I breathed a sigh of relief. *It was good to get out of Nairobi.*

Two and a half hours after leaving the city we entered Hell's Gate, where open terrain spotted with baobabs and acacias gave way to towering cliffs and looming rock formations. We drove slowly through the grassy plains, sheltered on either side by the craggy stone. Colorful birds soared overhead, their plumage so vivid that watching them, we almost drove into a herd of zebra.

The zebra were oblivious to our presence, unlike the pack of baboons that came right up to the vehicle, jumping on the hood of the car to get a better look at us.

Tano turned off the engine so we could study them more closely. They were curious beasts, with their hairy homo sapiens-like bodies, long, expressive faces, and close-set eyes. They might have been appealing, were it not for the sight of their big pink behinds that protruded obscenely.

I wasn't going to comment but when one of the males pressed his hairless flamingo colored bum against the window, I couldn't refrain. "Gross!"

Tano turned on the ignition. "We can park at the gorge and walk."

Walk? I glanced over to see if he was joking.

"Tano, the last thing I want to do is go strolling through this park. We have no idea *what's* out there…"

"You're afraid of zebras?"

His tone indicated this to be utterly ridiculous, but as a matter of fact, I *was* afraid of zebras…and those icky baboons. Not to mention all the other unknown beings we could potentially cross.

The sense of threat I felt prevented me from budging on the hiking idea, but I agreed to pitch our tent in one of the designated sites, up on a hill looking out over the park. This way I could keep watch,

I figured. And we were close enough to the car that we could make a run for it if need be.

Fortunately, the night was uneventful, and the following morning I hugged Tano from behind as he peeled the juicy, sweet pineapple we'd bought on the road to Naivasha. We were organizing breakfast out of the trunk of the car, dipping into the supplies that we had stored there overnight. The bananas had ripened to a beautiful hue, and as I peeled one slowly, looking out over the exhilarating landscape, I said, "This has been *so* relaxing."

Then I spotted the heads in the brush.

"Oh my God!"

Twenty snarling, yipping baboons, some as large as wolves, came charging at us. Within seconds we were surrounded.

One of the largest - clearly male, his big penis standing out prominently – was the first to lunge, straight for our pineapple.

Tano grabbed two dead branches and swung them in the air as I ran for the tent.

Through the flimsy nylon netted window, I watched more baboons charge for the bananas. Yellow peels and soft fleshy fruit flew through the air.

"Help me!" Tano shouted, yanking the door of the tent open. He shoved a branch into my hand. "I'm going to get those bananas back! You guard the cookies!"

He ran up the hill, towards the mama baboon perched on a stump with her baby, holding a banana and looking at him with an expression of bored curiosity.

Finished with their snack, three of the baboons inched down the hillside towards me. The trunk of the car was still wide open, the cookies scattered there in a crumbly mess.

"Don't just stand there!" Tano shouted, "Close the trunk!"

But when the trio pounced, I dropped the branch and ran screaming to the tent.

Tano galloped back toward our camp, still swinging the branch, just as the big bully who had devoured our pineapple came behind him in a beeline for the kettle. This time it was the baboon who screamed as he grabbed the handle, discovering - as his palm sizzled - that it was burning hot. He dropped it and retreated at high speed up the hill – little comfort to us, since his cronies right behind him had eaten every last one of our cookies.

"Why didn't you defend us?" Tano demanded. He looked like a wild-eyed bushman, club in hand, crazed expression on his face.

I couldn't hold back my laughter.

But he didn't see the humor. "How could you just let them do that to us?"

I ignored his question, scanning the landscape for any lingering beasts. But Tano forlornly plucked the upended kettle from the coals.

"If you had helped me we could have saved the cookies."

I stared at him, debating my response. But silence was all I could manage, engulfed in the realization of just how different we really were.

In late autumn, the El Niño rains brought an epidemic to the Rift Valley. Several family members of a wealthy clan chief came down with high fever and diarrhea. They were taken to a hospital, but instead of getting better with IV medications, they all died, within hours of each other, bleeding from their noses and eyes – the sure sign of hemorrhagic fever. The nurses who cared for this family came down with the same symptoms a few days later and also died.

The day Tano left to investigate, Mama Florence arrived at work with another phone message:

PROFESSIONAL WOMEN'S NETWORKING DINNER
TONIGHT 7:30 P.M. AT ADDIS ABABA RESTAURANT.
ALL WELCOME, NO RSVP REQUIRED

Professional women? Did I qualify?

Charles dropped me off at the restaurant that evening. From the moment I walked in, it was clear who I was looking for. Seated around a large table were eleven women, all *muzungus,* and by the sound of their boisterous voices, American.

I approached tentatively. "Is this the professional women's group?"

"Not for tonight, honey!" one of the women shouted from the far end of the table, waving a bottle of beer. Everyone howled with laughter.

"Are you a professional woman?" someone asked.

"I'm trying to be."

Everyone tittered again, and the woman closest to me scooted over on the bench so I could sit down. I was introduced around the table and someone handed me a glass of *tesch*, Ethiopian honey wine, with the warning that it was potent stuff.

The woman I was sitting beside was blusterous and jolly, her long grey hair hanging halfway down her back in a sort of loose, ex-hippie style. She looked about sixty-five, with huge eyes and an angular, stork-like frame, her tiny waist cinched by a three-inch-wide belt fastened with a big orange bauble. A chunky stone necklace in matching orange sat, unmoving - in spite of her vivacious body language - in the middle of her bony chest.

Her name was Phyllis Cooble, and from the way she dominated the group it was clear she was the Alpha Female. Relaxing as the *tesch* went to my head, I asked her what she was doing in Nairobi.

"I'm with USAID. Been with 'em my whole career. You're not that new girl in Admin, are you?"

"No, I'm not with USAID," I said. "Although I did loads of Summer Hire when I was a teenager."

"Summer Hire" was a State Department program designed to give children of diplomats an opportunity to work during school holidays. In practice, we mostly played cards in each other's offices, or took advantage of innumerable opportunities for hilarity, such as photocopying our faces and faxing them to our friends.

"*Ohhhh*," Phyllis said knowingly. "You're a diplomatic brat."

Abruptly I had a sense of being on the "inside" – one of the club.

I ran down the list of my father's postings, each one obviously making Phyllis more confident that I was a "professional woman" - one of them.

"And what brings you to Nairobi?"

"My husband works for MSF."

"Ah-hah," she said. "He's a cowboy, and you're alone most of the time?"

Cowboy? I privately mused. *Hard-working, hard-living, completely self-sufficient, and totally fearless?* Yes, it actually summed up Tano perfectly.

"So what *do* you do?" Phyllis asked.

"I'm a clinical social worker. And I also have a master's degree in Public Health."

"Working?"

"Part-time. I'm volunteering. As a counselor at the Teenage Clinic at Kenyatta Hospital."

"So we're all one big happy family! We fund that clinic, you know."

"Yes, I know." I wondered if I should bring up the lamentable dearth of folders. I decided to first get more information. "What do you do, Phyllis?"

"I work on bilateral initiatives that focus on capacity building and quality control of delivery of services in under-served and crisis-laden high risk areas."

Her description was straight out of the development jargon handbook. I barely understood what she'd just said.

Seeing my confusion, she lowered her voice, "I mostly plan meetings. I'm the gal at USAID that gets stakeholders together to *talk*."

Stakeholders?

But before I could ask, she said, "So what do you do when you aren't helping out at Kenyatta?"

"Mainly look for another job."

"Come and work for me," she said abruptly. "I could use some help."

"Really?"

"Yep. I'll take you on as a consultant."

I smiled. It was as easy as my professor had said.

"Come to my office tomorrow," Phyllis said, drawing a little map on the back of her business card. "11 AM?"

"OK," I agreed, already feeling drunk as Phyllis clinked her glass to mine.

"Drink up ladies!" she called to the crowd, as though we were sorority sisters. "We've got a new recruit! To Africa!"

The following day Mama Florence pointed me in the direction of Parklands, on the other side of Westlands, where USAID was situated. I set off on foot, down Rhapta Road with all its luxuriant foliage, to the Westlands Roundabout with its garbage piles and glue sniffers, past the flower vendors, the *mitumba*, and the vegetable market.

After that, everything was new. I passed a funny lotus-shaped structure that said "Meditation Center," and a run down building marked "Police Station". The charred and mangled remains of two *matatus* stood in front of it. Thank heaven I didn't need to rely on them any longer, with Charles on call.

Ten minutes later, I arrived at a tall stone building in a shady enclave. The United States Agency for International Development.

Showing my US passport got me through the security barriers with ease, and I entered the depths of USAID. In contrast to the urgency of MSF and the intensity of Kenyatta Hospital, USAID presented a calm sterility.

On the sixth floor, I sat across the desk from Phyllis, dressed today in a red and yellow tie-dyed boo-boo which made her look even more like the den mother in a hippie commune. On her desk was a little bowl of candy corns.

She pushed them towards me. "My weakness," she said. "Help yourself. They just got a shipment in at the commissary and I stocked up."

My mind flashed back over the different Embassy commissaries of my childhood. Flying in candy corn – and other such important food products - was one of the perks the US government provided its official communities abroad.

"Before I forget," Phyllis said, lowering her voice conspiratorially, "Here." From under her desk she pulled out a plastic shopping bag. Glancing dramatically in all directions, as though we were being watched, she slid the bag across the table at me.

Folders. As the bottle of tesch had circulated I had revealed the plight of the filing system. I started to thank her but she abruptly changed the subject.

"Now let's talk turkey. What's your daily rate?"

My daily rate?

"To be honest, Phyllis, I've never been asked the question."

She leaned back and smiled. "Rule number one, honey. In this business, never admit your inexperience."

I lowered my voice. "But I *am* inexperienced."

She held out her hand – *STOP* - as though she were a traffic cop. "I can offer you $110 a day."

I was taken aback. At $110 per day, I'd be making twice as much as Tano. *No more debates about the price of cappuccinos!*

"Well...yes, OK. Thanks."

"It will just be a chunk of change at the end of every month." She flashed me a confident smile and winked. "But we'll augment it, of course, over time."

Forty five minutes later, I left USAID with an income, the bag of folders, and a new title: *Consultant*.

But consulted on *what*, exactly? The more Phyllis had explained, the more nebulous it sounded. With no training in development work, I could only guess what she meant by "providing technical assistance" and "performing data analysis."

The one term I'd managed to clarify was "stakeholders" - the people for whom Phyllis, with my help, was to plan meetings. Apparently this meant anyone that got money from USAID. Government officials. Ministers of Health. Politicians. Not the lowly and harassed frontline workers at places like the Teenage Clinic, but the top people who dispensed the funds that eventually trickled down to them if they were lucky.

I walked slowly back towards Westlands. What did a consultant *look* like? I envisioned a confident woman in an impeccably pressed safari suit striding into USAID's board room, serious leather brief case in hand.

"Technically speaking, this is what I think we should do."

The fantasy stopped there. Beyond the image I just couldn't conjure any content.

And I was supposed to start work on Monday. I wished Tano was here to tell me what a consultant was supposed to *do*, what the hell I was supposed to analyze…Although even if I looked forward to announcing my salary, I didn't relish the idea of revealing that the job I'd landed was at the evil USAID.

At the Westlands *mitumba*, I decided to browse for something a consultant might wear. But it was a silky kimono that finally caught my eye, its royal-blue fabric shimmering in the sunlight, giving life to the fire-flaring dragon embroidered on the back.

The vendor saw me looking. "400 shillings, Madam."

I hesitated. 400 shillings was almost one round trip to Kenyatta in Charles' decrepit cab. But now I had a *real* salary...

A group of *muzungus* piling out of a tourist taxi and heading towards the stalls decided for me.

"I'll take it."

As he put the kimono in a plastic bag, a car pulled up. My heart rate quickened when I saw who it was.

Guillaume. *Shit.*

I shoved the kimono in my purse. God forbid that *he* should see me buying something so frivolous while he and my husband were trying to stop an epidemic.

"You need a lift?"

I hesitated for a second. We had never been alone together, and I actually would have preferred to just keep walking. But the offer of a ride implied an olive branch.

"OK, thanks." I climbed in the car. As he pulled into traffic he said, "Tano is coming back tonight."

"He is?"

It was the first time Guillaume had conveyed anything like personal information to me. Truthfully, I sometimes thought of him as an ant, tirelessly working and only sharing information with other ants in the colony – not the pretty but useless butterfly. Assuming it was as a butterfly he saw me, and not just a brainless grasshopper.

But any hope of a crack in his armor disappeared when he continued, "Yes. More people have died. We've just confirmed Rift Valley Fever. And there is also *fameen*."

"Fameen?" *What was that?*

"The cows and goats were hit before the human population," he said as he accelerated up Rhapta Road. "With the animals dead the people have no food. There has been *fameen* for several months."

Famine. People were starving.

"What are you going to do?"

"We are preparing an emergency feeding intervention alongside the epidemic control. A team is on their way from Paris."

We had arrived back at MSF. Guillaume stopped the car, brusquely, in the middle of Rhapta Road so that I could get out in front of our apartment building.

"Thank you, Guillaume. For the ride. And the... er, briefing."

He nodded curtly as I climbed out of the car. I had already turned away when he called through the window, "He'll be back in the late afternoon."

Climbing the stairs, I wondered why he'd told me exactly when Tano would return. I felt a little as a divorced parent must, sharing custody of a child. *You can have him for this evening, but first thing tomorrow, he will belong to us once more.*

I kept watch from the balcony of our apartment. Finally at 5:30 the Land Rover with the MSF flag arrived at the gate across the street. Tano got out, waving and crossing the street toward me.

I ran down the stairs to meet him but stopped abruptly as he approached. He was holding a cool box. It was the exact same shape as the cheerful red ones of my childhood, in which we carried soda and sandwiches on picnics, but this one was grey and battered, marked with the MSF logo and the ominous words: HAZARDOUS MEDICAL SAMPLES.

"Is it safe to touch you?" I asked, my mind filled with visions of the two of us dead in each others arms, blood streaming from our bodily orifices.

"It's fine," he replied, setting the box down.

I threw myself into his arms. "I missed you."

He held me tightly - for a moment. Then he loosened his grip. "I have to get these blood samples to the lab. And check in at the office."

"And *I* have something to tell *you*."

"Can it wait? I need to discuss the plans...." He fidgeted, looking over his shoulder.

"They're preparing an emergency feeding intervention alongside the epidemic control," I parroted Guillaume. "A team is on the way from Paris."

Tano was startled. "So I heard. How did...?"

"Guillaume," I wrapped my arms around his neck again and whispered, "So now you know the plan. Come upstairs so *we* can catch up. Just for a minute."

He pried my arms away. "I can't. The team leaves for the Rift Valley early tomorrow and I need to brief them."

Although his explanation was perfectly legitimate, and one that a mature person would have accepted instantly given the gravity of the situation, I was not that evolved...and so I pouted, a useless means to no end, as confirmed by his next statement:

"And I'm going to Nyanza tomorrow."

"But you just got home!"

"Well, there are some problems with the treatment protocol and we've already got patients enrolled for anti-retrovirals."

He kissed me in a perfunctory, *I'm in a big rush* kind of way. "I'll come as soon as I can."

Puttering around the apartment in the early evening, I envisaged a full seduction upon Tano's return, sex still being my preferred mechanism for clinging on to him. By now, though, my confidence was shaken, the promise of sex not working with Tano any more than money was working with Africa.

But I wouldn't give up that easily. A bottle of white wine was chilling in the fridge and I had put sexy black lingerie on under the new blue kimono, still just a tiny bit damp from being washed.

But it wasn't until 10:30 that his key finally turned in the door. I jumped up at the sound.

"Hi." He smiled wearily, and then stared, as though I were standing before him in a clown suit. "What are you *wearing*?"

I pulled the kimono tightly around me. "Where were you?"

"Work."

"This late?"

The weariness on his face was replaced with irritation. "People are *dying* in the Rift Valley. I was briefing the team."

"It's just that I've been waiting all day to tell you," I stammered. "I got a job. A *paying* job."

"Congratulations," he huffed, although he looked surprised. "Where?"

"At USAID."

He raised his eyebrows.

"I'm just going to do it until I find something else."

We stood at a distance, like two dogs that had circled each other and decided not to fight. I finally told him about Phyllis Cooble and my daily rate, but didn't bother asking his advice about being a consultant. I felt idiotic enough already.

Then he said, "There's a dinner tonight. At Fabienne's. She is preparing *boeuf bourguignon*."

My breath caught in my throat. I wanted to scream and cry and rip my clothes off and try to sex him back to attentiveness. But the image of myself sitting there alone all evening in that ridiculous black underwear filled me with shame, the humiliation of waiting around for a man who had other things on his mind.

"Fine. We'll go to the dinner. I'll change my clothes."

In the bedroom I sat on the edge of the bed, my skin tingling with a sense of self-sabotage.

I hadn't even wanted to have sex. I just wanted *him* to want *me*.

I felt like I had lost all my power.

I took off the kimono and shoved it into a drawer.

I needn't have worried so much about my duties as a consultant. By the end of my first week on the job it was apparent that "consultant" was just a fancy way of framing the depressing truth:

I had become Phyllis Cooble's administrative assistant.

My first assignment involved helping her prepare for a meeting on "food security," a development term that referred to a population's access to enough food to secure a healthy and active life. Seven weeks from my first day of work, delegations would be arriving from Washington and twelve different African countries. They would all stay in a five star hotel in downtown Nairobi and spend three days eating, drinking, and talking about hunger.

"I need you to book rooms for every person on this list," Phyllis said, handing me several sheets of paper. "Then follow up with anyone who booked their *own* plane tickets. Make sure we know their arrival time so that you can plan their transport from the airport."

I appreciated how Phyllis had taken me under her wing, and had continued to slip me supplies from USAID's stocks – the clinic at Kenyatta now had a functional filing system *and* a small arsenal of ballpoint pens that seemed to disappear as quickly as I could supply them. But booking hotel rooms? Organizing airport shuttles? It felt like a glorified Summer Hire.

At the end of my first week, I complained to Tano. "The work plan made it sound so much more interesting."

Having realized how much paid employment boosted my self-esteem, he made an effort to be supportive. "I suppose booking hotel rooms *is* 'providing technical assistance'. Although I still don't understand the 'data analysis' part."

I found out the next morning.

"About the gala banquet," Phyllis said the moment I walked into the office. "Do you think more people will want fish or meat?"

"Ummmm…"

"Let's not speculate," she said. "Call everyone, and find out if they want Tilapia or beef the last night of the meeting. The ministers from Botswana and Lesotho – now *they* are fish men. But Minister Kazibwe, from Uganda? Steak all the way…"

I tried not to groan, imagining the day ahead of me, struggling with the decrepit intercontinental telephone system just to ask what so and so wanted for dinner.

"When you've got the info, call it into the hotel chef. And when you do, don't forget to order those *delicious* hors d'oeuvres I told you about– the ones with cucumber? The Minister from Malawi was so fond of those the last time we had him to Nairobi."

The weeks passed and my two worlds diverged even more radically. Mondays, Wednesdays and Fridays I supervised hors d'oeuvres for "stakeholders," Tuesdays and Thursdays were spent in my broom closet at Kenyatta, facing problems that ranged from the absurd – a father enquiring about the modern day use of chastity belts for his daughter – to the devastating, the details of each story changing but the substance generally some variation on sexual abuse and HIV infection.

One afternoon, two weeks before the food security meeting, Phyllis buzzed me on the interagency line.

"Come quickly. There's an emergency."

I raced down the hallway to her office. She waved for me to sit down.

"The key rings are all wrong."

The key rings were one of the "take-aways" Phyllis gave out at every conference. Just a few weeks earlier, we'd spent several hours discussing whether we should order the damn things in indigo or turquoise. I'd found it banal...until I saw the invoice for these party favors. The budget far surpassed what most clients who came through the Kenyatta clinic could hope to see in a year.

"The pen sets are OK," Phyllis said, "and the tie-dye folders are gorgeous, but the key rings..." She shook her head as though it were too painful to say more. "We should never have ordered the turquoise," she said. "Too risqué. I've just called for a driver to take you to the supplier to sort this out."

"Phyllis, really...Does it matter?"

"These things may seem like just a silly detail, honey. But they make *all* the difference to our participants." A reflective look came over her face. "*This* is how we solidify collaboration with foreign governments. *This* is how democracy spreads."

I took the offending turquoise key ring and went downstairs to wait for the driver. *Ask not what your country can do for you, but what you can do for your country....*

Two days before the meeting, Phyllis called me into her office again, in another panic.

"I need you to organize the per diem." She handed me a box. It was filled with US banknotes. "Prepare envelopes for each participant. This is the breakdown." She flashed a list that detailed how many hundreds, fifties and twenties went into each envelope, depending on how long a participant was going to be in Nairobi.

"What's the money for?"

"To offset their costs."

"What costs? We pay for the hotel rooms and plane tickets, and all the meals are catered."

Phyllis shot me a look. Apparently this was not an appropriate question.

I bristled as I stuffed banknotes into envelopes. I should take the money and run. I imagined the look on the faces of some of those teenage prostitutes if I were to hand them even a fraction of this much money. Lord knew they were the ones - not the African Ministers and the big shots from Washington - that really needed the handouts.

Then I blew it at the Teenage Clinic.

I'd gone in to work one day to find a message from Doctor Muthaiga, the hospital executive, awaiting me at the reception.

"Go quickly," Sister Gladys said, a grave look on her face.

I hurried down the hospital corridors to his office.

Dr. Muthaiga, a distinguished older man with graying hair and thick glasses, went straight to the point.

"What do you think you are doing here, young girl?"

Intimidated by his ominous tone, I just gaped.

"You can cause us to lose our funding!" His voice rose as he pulled a stack of folders out from under his desk and tossed them in my direction. They scattered as they hit the surface of his desk, and I cringed at the sight of my handwriting.

"You beg folders from the boss at USAID? What message does that give about us? We have a budget for folders. If you needed them, you should have come to me."

"Sister Gladys said...."

"Sister Gladys will be reprimanded," he snapped. "And I suggest you think carefully if it is a good idea for you to continue on here. Now you are dismissed."

I left Kenyatta with my head hanging. How could I have been so naïve? It all seemed so idiotic now, thinking that improving the filing system would make any difference. It all came back to money: how to get it and keep it.

But the following day when I played my encounter with Dr. Muthaiga back to Phyllis, she laughed. "He won't lose his funding over that, for God's sake. But let it be a lesson in capacity building."

"Capacity building" was another favorite term in development-speak that referred to building up skills within an institution so as to upgrade the quality of service.

Phyllis was cheerful because the food security meeting had gone off without a hitch. A good time had been had by all, and the participants were back home with their complimentary key rings and other gifts, as well as their unearned *per diems*. Had anything been accomplished toward improving food security? I seriously wondered.

But we were already talking about our next endeavor: the "Embrace All of Africa" desk agenda, concocted as a token of goodwill from the US government to its stakeholders. Thousands of dollars had been budgeted for its creation. A graphic designer from the United States had even been pulled on board as another consultant.

My onerous task was to track down the birthdays of dozens of government dignitaries from every African country that had ever participated in EAI programs. The birthdays of each would appear in the desk agenda.

Hours were spent calling Ministries of Health all over sub-Saharan Africa. I was lucky if I only had to dial a number nine or ten times before being connected, and even luckier if I found the person I was looking for. Some countries were so hard to reach that I ended up having to e-mail the USAID missions.

It was embarrassing.

Dear so and so,

I am a consultant at USAID in Nairobi. Could you please find out the birthday of the Minister of Health?

I was brooding over this silly desk agenda as I washed the dishes one evening after a simple plate of *sukuma wiki* and *ugali.*

The post-dusk stillness was broken by the squealing of tires on pavement, loud and startling, followed by the sound of an engine revving. Then, a woman's screams.

I ran to the balcony. Down below, I saw two white cars stopped at odd angles in the middle of the street. Suddenly the door of one opened violently, and a woman, a *muzungu,* tumbled into the dusty road. She screamed again, a shrill noise punctuated only by a few words. "Help me! Somebody help me!"

Gunshots popped over her cries as she pounded on the gate of our compound. The guard yanked her in by the arm, barely cracking open the gate, the white of her blouse and her blonde hair a flash in the dim. The bolt clicked shut as the two cars peeled off into the night.

I ran down the stairs. The woman was already surrounded by the men in our building who had made it down first. When she saw me, the only other female, she reached out and grabbed me by the forearms.

"I wit my pents!" she sobbed in a heavy South African accent. She had a wild look on her face as she gestured to the big wet stain creeping up the back of her beige skirt. "I wit my pents!"

The whole compound was charged with fear. Everyone was talking at once, complimenting the woman for escaping, thanking God that the bullets had not hit her, cursing the mafia that was behind this violence, comparing stories of when it had happened to them, or their boss, or their friends.

The woman latched back onto my arms. "I feel faint."

"Sit," I said, helping her to the curb. She put her head on her knees.

One of the *muindi* neighbors had a phone and was trying to call the police.

"Why bother?" Someone asked. "You think they will come?"

"It was probably the police themselves," another remarked.

"Please," the *muzungu* said, "Can I call my boyfriend?"

We waited for him upstairs, sitting side by side on the sofa.

"In Jo'burg they just kill you and then take the car." Her face was ashen. "I feel lucky."

"You're extremely brave. I don't know if I would have dared jump out of the car."

"I think they were going to rape me."

I shuddered.

"I would have rather been shot than gang raped," she whispered.

I put my arm around her and we sat like that until her boyfriend arrived. I could hear him verbally abusing the guards as he entered the compound and then his footsteps as he bounded up the stairs, two, three at a time.

"Darling?" he shouted as he approached. "Darling?"

I opened the door and he came bursting through, masculine and super-heroic. I watched as he took her into his arms, caressing her hair and making soothing noises into her ear. We spoke for only a few moments and then they left.

I closed all the windows, locked the front door, and pushed the sofa up against it. Then I wrapped myself in a blanket and perched on the edge of the sofa. I couldn't stop trembling, couldn't slow the replay coursing through my mind: the screams, the flash of the woman's hair in the dark, the sound of gunshots...

I couldn't sleep. *Wouldn't* sleep. How could I? What if the carjackers came back? Keeping watch was imperative, now that I knew what lurked outside in the Nairobi night. It was something more threatening than I had ever imagined.

I must have fallen asleep, because a beam of sunlight awoke me with a start, its radiance mocking my bleak mood. I splashed water on my face and went to MSF to tell them what had happened.

But when I got there I discovered the team in a flurry. Pierre, the logistics officer and his Kenyan girlfriend, Mary, had also been carjacked the night before along Rhapta Road. They were telling their story to Guillaume and Fabienne when I walked in. The carjackers had tried to molest Mary as well, but she had managed to talk them out of it.

"It's such a horrible coincidence," I said, feeling more shaken with every new piece of information.

"Not such a coincidence," Guillaume said. "Rhapta Road has always been dangerous - it's not lit and has multiple access points to the highway."

"And the carjackers are looking for unmarked white Toyota sedans these days," Fabienne added. "The Westlands Roundabout is a hangout for thugs. They must have been waiting there and following people."

My trepidation abruptly boiled over to anger.

"Then why on earth are the office and our housing on Rhapta Road? And why do you all drive white Toyotas?"

"Crime is everywhere in Nairobi," Guillaume shrugged. His tone was rational, devoid of panic. "And white Toyotas happen to be in vogue now, but in a few months the carjack mafia will favor something else. *Alors....*"

He turned to Fabienne, the discussion of carjacking closed as far as he was concerned. "Are we ready to leave?"

Seeing my confusion, Fabienne said, "There is a cholera outbreak on the coast. We will have to send Tano."

"When is he coming back?" I wailed.

"He'll be here tonight," she said, sipping some water. "But he'll have to leave first thing in the morning."

Could they tell I was about to start bawling?

She put her hand on my arm, as though to steady me. "There's a political complication. It was the Catholic church of Mombasa that alerted us about the epidemic. The Kenyan government is denying the presence of the disease."

"Why would they--?"

"*C'est evident,*" she said, lighting the fifth cigarette she'd smoked since I'd walked into the office twenty minutes earlier. "The coast survives on tourism. Even the *word* 'cholera' has the potential to scare off visitors."

She took several drags.

"Once the Ministry of Health agrees that the epidemic exists, we'll need everyone." She took a final deep drag before stubbing the cigarette out in the ashtray. "As it is, the slums of Mombasa may become death camps."

When Tano's key turned in the lock that evening, I ran across the room to meet him at the door.

"Did you hear what happened? Did you hear about the carjackings?"

"*Hola, mi amor.*" He leaned to kiss me, but I turned my face with such evident distaste that he pulled back.

"I'll wash up. I'm covered with dust."

I followed him into the bathroom a moment later. "So, *did* you?"

He was lathering his face and didn't answer. Once he hung up the towel, he put his arms round my waist.

"I did. Thank God no one was hurt. Now can I kiss you?"

I offered forth my lips but my mind was still filled with the screeching of tires.

"Mmmmmm," he murmured. "You look good."

These words, which once would have been music to my ears, the ultimate promise of his devotion, now felt like a dismissal. I wanted to *talk*.

"It was awful," I said. "I just can't stop thinking about it. The sound of that woman screaming...."

He wasn't listening. Instead, he began peeling off my clothes. I watched as if from a distance as they dropped to the floor, not even feigning interest, connected only to my outrage as he made love to me. He'd done a poor job of washing his neck and his forearms beyond the wrist, and I tried to ignore what germs that dusty layer might carry.

When the act was over, I pushed him off of me, but full of postcoital tenderness he tried to fold me back into his arms.

"You wouldn't be feeling so good if I'd been raped or murdered."

He looked at me through narrowed eyes. "What are you talking about?"

"It was awful being here alone last night. I was terrified."

"Why? You're safe in this apartment."

"Oh really?"

"There's a good lock on the door, and we're up on the third floor. What else do you need?"

He left the room and a few seconds later the light in the kitchen blinked on. I went to find him. He was leaning against the kitchen counter, drinking milk from the carton. Naked and dirty. I glared at him: *some comfort he was.*

Crumpling the now-empty milk carton, he said, "Shall we have dinner out tonight?"

"In our white Toyota? To attract the carjackers?"

"Don't exaggerate, *Querida*. It's a question of probability. It's *extremely* unlikely...."

I slapped my hands over my ears, refusing to let him assess our security statistically, like a virus. *"Please.* I want to stay home tonight. I'll make something. And no offense - you need a shower."

He grinned as though I was trying to be funny. "First I will go to the office. I'll be back in half an hour."

I sat there for a moment after he left, and then ran out to the balcony. In the dark I could barely see his back crossing the street. The fear of being alone in the night invaded me like an infection.

By sunrise the following day, Tano was already en route to Mombasa with the cholera team that had arrived from Paris. In the weeks that followed, I struggled with my fear of the night. But no matter how uneventful the day, sunset was the signal for the same unease to stealthily take over. I kept all the lights on, closed the windows, made sure the door was locked. Still, I barely slept.

I couldn't ask Tano to come home just because I was scared, especially because the epidemic that had exploded in the slums of Mombasa had already moved up the northern coast to Malindi. But when he'd been gone for a week, I broke down and called him from the MSF office. I had a legitimate excuse: Christmas was only ten days away.

"When are you coming back?"

"It's not clear."

An image of cutting into a Christmas turkey with Guillaume flashed before me. "Well what about the holidays?"

"There is a *cholera* epidemic. Do you understand what that means?"

The exasperation in his voice made me combative, and five minutes later, after an increasingly acrimonious exchange, we hung up, and I stormed out of the office onto Rhapta Road. Stomping across the street towards the apartment, I was flooded with anger. But as I charged up the stairs to our apartment, fury at Tano turned to intense self-flagellation. Of course he couldn't walk away from the epidemic just to sit around drinking eggnog with me.

The sound of Mama Florence singing hymns on the other side of the door broke into my furious rumination. I couldn't bear to face her.

I slinked back down the stairs. Out on Rhapta Road I took several deep breaths. Any large scale solutions to this conundrum evaded me. But solving the Christmas riddle suddenly seemed easier.

If Tano couldn't come home, I'd go to him.

Heat.

It rose up and enveloped me as I stepped off the plane in Mombasa. An MSF driver was waiting in the arrivals hall, holding a piece of cardboard on which my name was clearly printed in Tano's handwriting. We drove through the heart of old Mombasa, where the evidence of Arab colonial rule was reflected in the elegant yet crumbling archways of the buildings. Slowing down as the road became more densely packed with pedestrians, donkeys, and *matatus*, the driver finally pulled over to a full stop.

"This is the cholera camp."

In the midst of this swirling urban scene stood a large structure made of corrugated iron, roofed in white canvas imprinted with the MSF logo. Kenyan watchmen stood guard at the entrance. They wore small jerry cans on their backs with long spray nozzles attached.

Each time someone came through the door from the inside, the guards sprayed their shoes. There was a strong smell of disinfectant.

I stood quietly inside, my eyes sweeping over the scene: Fifty or so beds were lined neatly in rows, each one filled. Before Tano had left Nairobi, he'd described the cholera cots, but I was still shocked by the sight of them: simple canvas beds with holes cut out at the level of the pelvis so that the patient's bare behind was exposed. Underneath the hole was a bucket to catch the liquid draining from their bodies. Some patients in the ward were also throwing up into buckets.

I had never seen so *much* sickness, never been confronted by this scale of suffering, punctuated by the utterly human sounds reverberating through the air: gagging, retching, moaning, and shitting…Fifty people at once, at different intervals and with no reserve. They were too sick to care.

Across the room, Tano was going from bed to bed, checking IVs, speaking quietly to the patients. When he saw me, he stopped what he was doing and came over.

"You made it," he spoke quietly. "I'm so happy you came."

I smiled, as happy to see him as I was to have asserted myself. "Me too."

But by common consent, we didn't touch.

"Do you want to see the ward?"

I nodded yes, and we walked back to where he had left off. Nurses wearing the same nozzled jerry cans patrolled the aisles, spraying between the cots.

"It is a bleach-water solution," Tano explained.

"That's all?"

"It's basic but effective. Just like the treatment."

He checked an IV line as he spoke. The old man in the bed looked wanly at us and closed his eyes. I thought he had drifted off to sleep but then he groaned, a deep aching noise. Liquid flushed into the bucket.

"You see, the cholera patient defecates – this painful, crampy diarrhea." Tano gestured to the old man, whose intestines were *still* draining out, "until there is no fluid left in the body."

In the next bed over a woman retched.

"Cholera kills fast - within one to two days. Dehydration causes a drop in temperature and blood pressure. The loss of sodium and potassium causes the vomiting. After that, coma and cardiac arrest." He held up the transparent tube dripping a solution into the patient's arm. "But if we replace the lost minerals and fluids like this, even a person near death has a good chance of recovering completely."

"Daktari!"

Voices rose by the main entrance of the ward.

"Daktari!"

It was a short, round nurse who'd been spraying the far end of the tent when I first walked in. She hurried in our direction, slow on heavy feet.

"Some parents are here. They want to take the body of the young girl who died this morning. But we have not yet disinfected."

"Start the process now. We cannot release the body until we've done it."

The nurse went in one direction and Tano started towards the door.

"What's going on?" I asked, infused with emotion, the sounds of illness pounding all around us. We had reached the door. Outside a woman chanted, her tear-streaked face raised to the sky, while her husband looked anguished over the shoulder of the guard who had prevented him from storming into the clinic.

Tano motioned for me to wash my hands alongside him. "When a patient dies the family dresses the body for burial. It's always the women who prepare the body, and these same women cook a meal for all the relatives who come to pay their respects."

The smell of chlorine wafted up from our hands. Tano began washing his a second time and gestured for me to do the same.

As we walked out of the ward, we stood with our shoes in two different pans of the same bleach solution. While the guard sprayed our feet Tano said, "Most of these people don't have running water, so they can't wash their hands. If *we* don't disinfect the bodies, one cholera funeral can cause at *least* ten new infections."

We escaped from the camp to the Sea Breezes Hotel, where the team had made their base of operations. From the name, I was expecting a pleasant seaside resort, the months at USAID having filled my head with visions of five star luxury. The sight of the rundown building was an abrupt reminder of the difference in the budgetary priorities of MSF.

We went straight to the restaurant, where we ordered the daily special: *ugali* with beans.

"I would have liked to have taken you to a better place for lunch," Tano said. He looked around at the empty restaurant with its spare furnishings and sticky table tops. Then he shrugged. "But time is limited."

The lines on his face showed he was exhausted and the reality of what he was dealing with – what MSF was dealing with – hit me hard. *This* was life and death. My "problems" -- *boo-hoo, I need attention* -- suddenly felt absurd.

Just then the waiter arrived at our table with an enormous blob of *ugali*…and a few beans on the side. We laughed at the sight of it.

"Can we have more beans, please?" Tano asked.

"Beans are finished, Sir."

"Is there any *sukuma*?" I asked.

"*Sukuma* finished also, Madam."

As we ate our dry *ugali*, I asked Tano if I might accompany him to the other camps that afternoon. But I knew even as I asked that it was not realistic: *Risk of spreading infection; ban on non-essential people.*

So while Tano went back to work, I spent the afternoon reading by the pool, which had green scum floating on top.

After the cholera epidemic had been halted, Tano spent several weeks in Nairobi. But much as I'd hated his absence, once he was back, I realized it was actually more stressful having him there. Since MSF always socialized as a group, it meant a return to the nightly *aperos,* Fabienne's expert but invariably filling dinners, well lubricated with wine, and, what was worse, the necessity to drive to them through the dark streets of Nairobi, which – in my mind at least – seethed with rapacious carjackers.

"Now you're back in Nairobi," I complained, back in my pre-cholera state of discontent, "but we have almost no time together."

"We see each other every night."

"With Guillaume, Fabienne and the rest. Why can't it ever be just the two of us?"

Then he caught me off guard. "We could try camping again this weekend, if you'd like."

But after the last time, I wasn't so sure.

"There's a private campground on Lake Naivasha," he pressed. "No baboons."

"You're sure?"

"Positive."

Muddy Banks was far more serene than its name implied, with a wide expanse of green stretching down to the shores of Lake Naivasha. We pitched our tent by the edge of the lake and spent the rest of the day relaxing on a blanket in the sun. The lake was ostensibly full of hippos, although that afternoon we didn't catch sight of a single one. But a sense of the "other" Kenya, the one famous for its wildlife was present in the variety of colorful, musical birds and black-and-white tailed colobus monkeys swinging above in the treetops, timid and tame compared to their aggressive relatives at Hell's Gate.

That evening in the campground's restaurant we ate grilled fish and drank cold beer, and had just ordered another round when the owner of Muddy Banks, a white Kenyan in a crisply starched safari suit came by our table and said, "Better if you take your last beers in the tent. Once the hippos appear it won't be safe to move from the restaurant."

I thought of the fat bumbling animals with their ever chewing jaws, their waddling walk, the odd habit of waggling their tails as they defecated to break up the turds – the basis of an African legend, that they did so to prove to the King of the Fishes that they had not eaten any of his subjects: *Look, no bones!*

How could hippos represent any threat?

"Hippos are like buffalo," Tano explained as we walked to the tent. "If they get spooked they will charge. But there shouldn't be anything to worry about in the campsite. It's probably just a precaution."

Back in the tent we reached out to each other, sealing our evening of rapprochement with a lingering kiss. Suddenly Tano pulled back.

"Listen!"

"Mmmmm?" I tried to pull him down on top of me.

"Shhhh!"

"What is--"

"Shhhh!"

I listened. Through the thin nylon of the tent I heard grunts, snorts and...loud munching noises?

"Hippos," he whispered. "I'm sure of it. I'm going to look."

Very carefully he sat up and unzipped the window panel of the tent.

He gasped. "We're *surrounded* by them. I can see six. They're grazing around the tent."

I got up on my knees and looked. It was true. Six enormous grey beasts loomed within a meter of us, peacefully chomping away on the grass that we had so casually lounged on just a few hours earlier.

"This is terrible," he whispered. "We could be trampled to death."

"Relax." I tried to put my arms around him, but at that moment one side of the tent went concave as a body grazed up against it.

"*A LA MIERDA!*" Tano's face was covered with sweat.

"It's going to be OK," I said, surprised at how calm *I* felt. For some reason the hippos didn't faze me. Unlike baboons – and their homo sapiens relatives –they didn't *want* something from us. They were naturally territorial, true, but they just wanted to graze in peace. The kind of animal I knew how to handle.

We stayed awake the rest of the night, Tano keeping watch out the window, me rubbing his back. I was filled with an astounding sense of courage, keeping a steady watch over him as he kept up a skittish surveillance of the hippos.

As daylight came, the mammoth beasts lumbered slowly back towards the lake.

"They're all back in the water," said Tano. "*Gracias a Dios.*" He lay back and blew his breath out.

It was the first time I'd ever seen him scared. I couldn't help but note how much I'd enjoyed being the brave one. I stretched out next to Tano and said a silent 'thank you' to the hippos for providing me the chance to play that role.

As time passed I began to feel like Tano and I were on a system of pulleys: the busier he got with MSF, the more distance between us. The more I admired (and envied) his work, the less connected I felt to him emotionally. I suspected he felt some inverse of the same...not that he cared to discuss such matters.

It would have made a good paper for some congress of social workers. *Patterns of Marital Alienation in Expatriate Aid Workers: A Comparative Study....* I smirked at the fantasy as I smoked a joint one evening, alone on the balcony, the lights of MSF burning brightly across the street.

But behind my smile was an ache, one that even the marijuana was not able to fully anesthetize.

From substance abuse counselor to substance abuser, I thought every time I lit a joint. But at least now I understood firsthand why people were driven to drink and drug.

The pot *consoled* me, helped me deal with the other things occupying my mind, mostly reflections about why I had signed on to this life which was so clearly not the one I wanted. Now, stuck here in scary Nairobi, thoughts about free will and sovereignty as a woman – once abstract concepts I had glibly written academic papers about in my *Politics of Patriarchy* class at Mount Holyoke – had crept back into my consciousness. Deep down I dreamed of leaving, but that was just not in my DNA: One did not leave one's husband. Period. The end.

So I continued to make feeble efforts at spicing things up. On Valentine's Day, Phyllis presented me with some duty-free wine. I called Tano from USAID to see if he wanted to stay in for dinner, just the two of us, to celebrate.

"But there is a party tonight," he answered.

"Guillaume wants to pass out candy hearts?"

"Very funny," he replied. "It's to welcome the new regional logistics coordinator. I think you'll like her. She's cool."

"Cool?" It had become clear these last months that his definition of cool did not necessarily match mine. "Cool how?"

"Does wearing rings on your toes count?"

Kavita, the new regional logistics coordinator, was not at all whom I'd been expecting to meet. A Kenyan Indian who had lived in Britain from the age of 15, she was exactly my age and had long black hair, wore thick kohl eyeliner and was strikingly beautiful, dressed in a silky *Salwar-Kamiz*, the Indian-style lounge set. And indeed, she had rings on her toes, fingers, and even her nose.

The usual crowd was there that evening, and when we arrived they were well into their drinks, the smell of marijuana already heavy in the air. Fabienne and Guillaume were sitting on the sofa in hot debate as always, while Pierre and Mary danced in the corner. There were six other people from the Paris office I did not know, and Tano joined them after he introduced me to Kavita.

"You don't work for MSF, do you?" Kavita's voice was sensual, the elegance of British English tempered with warm Indian melodiousness.

"No," I said, getting ready to apologize for my outsider status.

"*Thank God*. At least there's one person here that won't talk work."

I laughed.

"They're such a cultish group. You must get so fed up."

She lit the joint and listened intently as I recounted all the awkward months with the team and my various frustrations. Our rapport was instant and we hugged like old friends at the end of the evening, promising to meet again soon.

"Kavita is totally cool," I bubbled in the car on the way home. "Thank you so much for introducing us."

But Tano had something else to discuss.

"Guillaume needs us to move."

"What?"

"The apartment would make a very convenient guesthouse for MSF...so we are being moved to a *maisonette* down the road." *Maisonette* was French for little house.

"But I don't want to move. I like living in that apartment."

"Well, MSF needs it. But will it console you if I tell you that I have seen the *maisonette* and that it has a little garden? And a phone?"

Hearing that *did* console me, but I was mistrustful of the process that had brought us to this.

"What guarantee do we have that as soon as we get settled there Guillaume isn't going to move us all over again?"

"I doubt that will happen."

I sighed. "When do we move then?"

"Is tomorrow too soon?"

He didn't say it as if we had any choice.

The charm of the *maisonette*, one on a compound of twelve, made it hard to stay indignant. Our new home had two storeys and a little garden full of banana trees and a tall, flowering jacaranda.

And, as Tano had promised, there was a phone.

Never mind that the line was dead.

We could see the telephone wires from our back window. They were draped in a messy jumble off a wooden pole that stood erect in the center of the compound. Almost every day, the technicians, who wore white laboratory coats, could be spotted up top of the pole.

When were they going to fix it? I wondered. I soon found they weren't trying.

Kavita is the one that clued me in. Approximately fifty households shared the fifteen wires. If we wanted our line connected, all we had to do was pay the technician *kitu kidogo* - something small – and he would disconnect someone else's to plug in ours.

Well that was easy enough, I thought the first time I slipped a couple hundred shillings into the technician's hand. *The real meaning of 'capacity building' revealed...*

A few nights later Tano called his family in Argentina. When he got off the phone he commented, "The phone service isn't so bad. That was a good connection, and it's been working for several days now."

"Thanks to *kitu kidogo*."

He looked at me like I was crazy. "Have you been paying *bribes?*"

"Oh relax," I said, brushing past him. "I was sick of not having a phone...And besides I want to help the technicians." It was common knowledge that they, like most civil servants in Kenya, hadn't received their salaries for months.

Tano started to protest, but I held my hands over my ears. If we were in Kenya to help the poor, wasn't this as good a system as any?

In time, the relationship with the technicians became quite friendly. We would often wave to each other when one of them was up the pole, and I always secretly hoped that if I seemed benevolent enough they would leave our line turned on.

Having the phone proved very useful, now that I had a best friend to chat with. Kavita was as busy as Tano, but she always found time for a quick chat, "just to check in," and most evenings she popped by, before Tano came home, and before she went on to her next event, of which she always had many programmed. Her travel schedule was also as hectic as Tano's, so sometimes weeks would go by and I wouldn't see her. But I was always the first stop she made when she returned to Nairobi from the field.

"Our meetings ground me," she said.

Our meetings grounded me as well, and I guiltily confided to Kavita that I looked forward to seeing her more than I did my own husband.

"Shelve the guilt, girl," she replied breezily. "It's a purely western idea that your man is supposed to fulfill all your needs. In many parts of the world, the man exists just to protect, provide, and inseminate."

I laughed.

"Think of the harem," she added. "The women may all sleep with the same man, but they get their emotional needs met amongst themselves."

"Can we consider ourselves harem sisters?" I giggled. "Or co-wives?"

"Let's just stick with close girlfriends for now. I'm not sure I want to entertain the fantasy of sleeping with Tano on top of everything else I have to deal with."

I giggled again, traveling vicariously from Rwanda to Congo and back to Nairobi where Kavita had a long string of men – MSF, UN, and even a few stolid diplomats at the British High Commission – waiting on her hand and foot, all jealously and passionately in love with her. She played it cool with all of them – and with every update on her love life I found myself fantasizing being in her shoes, the faculty of seduction now but a distant memory.

One evening she came by, but instead of hunkering down for a chat, she begged me to go with her to the Gypsy, a bar a few minutes down the road that was the meeting place for expats from the NGO world.

Tano had been at the hospital in Nyanza all week and was coming home that evening, so I hesitated, saying I should be there to greet him. But with Kavita rolling a joint and rolling her eyes at the same time, I changed my mind.

"Lighten up, girl," she said. "Tano takes you for granted. Besides, I have to go to Sudan tomorrow and won't see you for weeks. So bless me with your company, please."

I left him a note, telling him where to find me.

We got to the Gypsy relatively early, but as it was a Friday night it was already packed. Loud jazz was playing and a small crowd of people were dancing in the middle of the room. The undercurrent was sexy and contagious and Kavita seemed to know half the men in the bar. She kept introducing me to the people who approached her, but the music was loud enough to just smile hello and not have to explain anything.

We moved through the crowd to an empty table and ordered *Dawas* - Kiswahili for medicine - a honey, vodka, and lemon drink that was a specialty in Kenya.

By the time the second drink coursed through my veins, I was out on the dance floor, grooving to the music with no one and everyone, flirting openly with the men that surrounded me, hypnotized by their attention and my renewed sense of freedom. Tano showed up as I was downing the last drops of my third *Dawa*. By then feeling irrepressibly high, any tension between us now drenched in alcohol and forgotten, I strutted my stuff across the floor. "Come on, honey! Let's dance!"

But just as I managed to get him to gyrate along with me, the thumping music slowed, and a melancholy horn carried over the din of the crowd.

"*Masquerade*! My favorite song." I snuggled up tightly against his chest.

Are we really happy in this lonely game we play? George Benson's sultry voice poured into the room.

We moved slowly in time to the music.

I could feel Tano's face grazing the top of my head, and I moved in closer, tightening my arms around his neck and closing my eyes. God, how I wanted *this*: Tano's undivided attention, his *response*.

It was just before midnight when the DJ pumped up the beat after a long string of slow songs. Tano and I left the Gypsy still entwined in each other's arms, stopping to kiss under a flickering street light. In the car, my hand rested possessively on his thigh as he steered towards the Westlands Roundabout. I leaned to nuzzle him as he drove, but suddenly he spoke, his voice as taut as when he'd first spotted the hippos.

"I think a car is following us."

I whipped around in my seat. Indeed, another white vehicle was on our tail. Inside I could make out the shapes of men.

Please God, no.

Our tires squealed as we rounded the corner onto Rhapta Road. I looked behind us again. The other car had turned on its high beams, the intense white light almost blinding.

I felt sick.

"Drive faster!"

The engine moaned at the pressure of Tano's foot on the pedal. The car behind us tapped our back fender.

"*La puta madre!* They are trying to run us off the road!"

Oh God, it's happening.

<p>
D</p>ays blurred into weeks. My life was overtaken by fear. I couldn't concentrate, certain that gangsters were all around, and that I would be raped and murdered if I let down my guard.

Night time was the worst. I'd drift off into troubled sleep only to awaken in a panic, crying from nightmares of men with guns pulling me from the car, men beating Tano over the head, men lurking in the shadows of my bedroom and creeping to the edge of my bed…

Years later, when I had long since left Nairobi, I would understand that I was in a state of acute post-traumatic stress that would unfortunately set the tone for the rest of my stay in East Africa. The symptoms were classic: anxiety, panic, flashbacks, nightmares…But at the time I couldn't recognize any of it. I was too close to the situation.

Ever immune, Tano had gone straight back to work the morning after the attack, sending the pulley system of our marriage into full swing. The more my mental function waned with each passing week, the further he seemed to disappear into his work. The more unavailable he became, the deeper I sank.

He thought my reaction was disproportionate. "Getting carjacked was bad, yes," he'd argue. "But many people go through far worse and they carry on with life."

"Except it could happen again, at any time."

"The probability of getting carjacked a second time is *minimal*. You're being irrational."

But each reference to rationality and probability just made it worse. So I did what any deeply miserable person who felt completely out of control would do: I waged a war on my husband, telling anyone who would listen how he just didn't "get" it. *Wasn't Nairobi awful, and wasn't my husband a total jerk for not understanding that?*

Time went on, and we fought – frequently and intensely. The mere suggestion of getting in the car after dark was torture. Did people not understand what we risked to get to their stupid parties?

But staying at home alone was just as harrowing. So sometimes I agreed to go out with him. When that happened, I would gasp at every car that pulled onto the road behind us, and while the sheer fright I felt at that time will always be real to me, it would be years before I could even begin to imagine what it must have been like for my fearless husband, trapped in the car with an insufflating basket case.

At some point, in an attempt to get my mind off carjacking, Tano took a few days off of work to whisk me almost 300 kilometers away to Masai Mara, Kenya's most famous wildlife reserve. We stayed in a fancy hotel and did the requisite game drives that came as part of the package. Indeed, the open plain was stunning, and the animals incredible to behold: hundreds of species, including the predatory leopard, cheetah and lion. My fragile state, however, made me more inclined towards their prey: the gazelle, topi and eland, who wore startled expressions that seemed to perfectly replicate my own.

A few nights after our return from Masai Mara, there was a *Nyama Choma* - a Kenyan barbeque - to say goodbye to Fabienne, who was leaving Nairobi for a mission in Haiti. I was seated on the other end of the table from Tano, next to a memorably handsome man named Jacques Rivière, who flirted openly with me throughout the meal. Charmed by his salt and pepper hair and quick smile, I managed to forget my worries for a moment to play along with his banter.

But my face went ashen when the discussion turned to the fact that the restaurant had been held up by gangsters just a week earlier. While everyone else tittered about the latest buzz word – *Nairobbery* – I ground my nails into the palms of my hands under the table.

"I can see you're upset," Jacques said quietly under the din, and I felt immediately self conscious. But before I could explain he added, "I heard about the carjacking. I'm so sorry. And I can understand why you're so weak."

He looked at me so kindly that I knew his assessment was not a slur or a judgment, but moreso a linguistic type of Freudian slip. But I stayed quiet until Tano and I were finally driving home. Then, between clenched teeth I said, "Why on earth did we go *there* tonight?"

"Probably safer than any place else we could have gone."

"According to your 'law of probabilities'?"

He didn't take the bait, and I bit my tongue, concentrating instead on scanning the streets for unspotted carjackers, a routine that involved rapidly pivoting my head - *Back! Front! Left! Right!* - sprung from some magical idea that if I was vigilant enough I could ward off any further attacks.

Once safely home, though, Tano sprawled comfortably on the sofa, reading *Le Monde,* I could no longer resist the urge to confront him.

"We need to leave Nairobi. Early, I mean. Before your contract is up."

He didn't even lower the newspaper. "Why? We just moved into this house."

"Because this is a *war zone*, Tano."

He peered at me from around the front page. "Have you ever seen a war zone?" He sounded amused. "Believe me, if you had, you'd appreciate what you have here."

The more cavalier he sounded, the more determined I became. "When I agreed to a life with MSF, you told me that we wouldn't have to live in dangerous places."

"This isn't dangerous – comparatively."

"And what if one of us gets killed?"

He lifted the newspaper again.

"We won't."

"How can you *know* that?"

Abruptly he dropped the paper to the floor, stood up and yawned. "I'm very tired. I'm going to bed."

I watched him leave the room, and I stood cemented in place, a tingling sensation running from the tips of my ears all the way down into my feet. I was strangely detached from the scene, as though I were circling above it, a mere celestial bystander to my own drama. But then the sounds of Tano performing his nighttime ablutions filtered down from the bathroom above, and I snapped back to attention, infused with a new burst of rage and indignation.

I charged up the stairs. He was already in the bedroom, standing in his underpants and fluffing his pillow.

"Don't you see how miserable I am?"

"Yes, I do."

"Do you even care?"

"I care enough to tell you that this can't go on. I think *you* should leave Nairobi."

Time froze. Suddenly, all I could picture was that moment of revelation in New Orleans.

The most important thing is that we stay together.

The city had worked its own voodoo, blinding me to all that could go wrong between two people from entirely different backgrounds. I was no longer even sure which gaps loomed largest: North and South American? Diplomatic child and MSF careerist? Woman and man?

We slept with our backs to each other. When morning came, I feigned sleep as he kissed my cheek goodbye, too depressed to face him. But once he was gone I pulled myself together and headed to the high security confines of USAID, where Phyllis' unflappable, maternal company acted like medication.

"You need to get yourself a big, black dog, Honey," she said over lunch a few hours later, seated in the USAID cafeteria. She was polishing off a double order of grilled cheese and fries, and I was barely choking down a dish of mashed potatoes.

"How will that help me feel safer when we go out?" I put my fork down, tears welling. I was getting used to bawling in front of Phyllis. It had been happening easily, without warning.

"You take the dog with you. Or hire a guard that will go with you everywhere. Or hell, do both. Safety in numbers."

A laugh escaped through my tears. There was no way Tano would *ever* agree to having some big smelly dog ride around in the car with us. And a personal guard too? I could only imagine him trying to explain that to the team.

"Or maybe you need to think about leaving Nairobi," she said. "I'd hate to see you go, but I'd understand."

I hadn't told her that Tano had suggested the exact same thing only a few hours earlier. It was too humiliating.

Because *obviously* I needed to leave. Family and friends back in the States, influenced by my long email tirades about living in a war zone with an insensitive jerk, had proposed the same. Yet it was not until ten years later, when a trusted friend read an original draft of this book, that anyone asked, "If he was such a jerk, why did you stay?"

The answer is not because I loved him, although that part is also true. But as I learned, "love" is not necessarily enough to keep people bonded together in times of great distress.

The answer is that I had no idea anymore who I was without him.

I may have resisted leaving the United States with Tano at first, but the vision of being the MSF doctor's wife had, finally, enticed me. Yet nothing had turned out as I had hoped, and I had lost so much confidence that more than ever I relied heavily on this pseudo identity.

Now with my marriage collapsing, and Tano unyielding in the face of my unhappiness, something had to give. It would be years before I was ready to take a full look at *my* role in my problems. Being the victim was always easier -- that way, the responsibility lay outside of myself. But given that he had just opened the door, I could no longer blame Tano for the fact that I was "stuck" in Nairobi.

Now I had to find a way to lie comfortably in this bed that I had made for myself.

Prozac. How easy it was. To obtain it. To pop a pill every morning with my coffee.

On the recommendation of a therapist friend in the States, I had dragged my depressed derriere to the Pharmacy at the Westlands Roundabout and secured a few hundred capsules. And suddenly, the bars of what I'd come to feel as a prison receded, and I began to actually accept my life in Nairobi. I approached my stint at USAID with a better attitude, spending chipper mornings promoting democracy by making nametags and ordering pen sets. Late afternoons I'd get home just in time to hear Mama Florence's eternally positive "Goodbye! I'm going back to the slum now!"

Then I'd lock the door and embark on the baking spree the antidepressant had triggered. Cakes, muffins, cookies…I prepared them compulsively, the act of following recipes providing the sense of order I craved, the sweet rise of dough providing the sense of accomplishment I needed. At some level I wanted to believe that the ingredients of my life could also fit together in this coherent a way, and like the treats I prepared, would eventually emerge, cooked to perfection, palatable.

When Tano returned from work, whenever it would be and regardless of who was with him, I would greet him with a barely contained ecstasy: I was *so glad* that he'd had an exciting day, *thrilled* that the team was joining us for dinner and especially delighted to offer round big hunks of cake, to the chorus of *mercis* from those I served.

People warmed to this version of me, especially Tano, who seemed just as elated to see me at the end of the day now, and who willingly went along with whatever I proposed, which was inevitably some variation on smoking joints (combined with the prozac the high was euphoric) and listening to loud acid jazz.

Every Sunday night from 7 to 10 a local radio station – Capital FM – hosted a jazz show with a smooth DJ named Jack Ojiambo, who started to feel like a good old friend so much I looked forward to those evenings with him, the volume on the radio turned way up while we boogied on down within the safety of our locked up house. Once the team had left, those jazzy moments with Tano turned quickly to lovemaking sessions on the sofa, followed by a last piece of cake before we'd stumble off to bed together.

One evening I was in the kitchen, making an angel food cake when Tano came home after ten days in Samburu land, the northern desert of Kenya. He had gone there to assess the situation after the Catholic Church had contacted MSF with reports of famine.

"Was it bad?" I asked, vigorously beating the egg whites.

"Very. We used the MUAC. The majority of the population is suffering acute malnutrition. We've already launched a therapeutic and blanket feeding."

By then I knew enough MSF jargon to translate. MUAC stood for Mid Upper Arm Circumference, and was a measuring tape graded in centimeters and colors, used to evaluate level of starvation. Children at risk of death fell in the red zone of the ribbon. Therapeutic feeding was for children near death. They had to be fed eight times per day with specialized food that contained minerals and vitamins. Blanket feeding was providing food rations to the entire community to prevent further malnutrition.

"A team from Paris has been on the ground since last week. I'm going back to work with them in a few days. Do you want to come with me?"

We left Nairobi a few days later, barreling out of the city in the early morning in a convoy of pick up trucks that carried supplies to stock the feeding centers. The highway was potholed and harrowing, with overburdened, lopsided lorries careening down the road at high speed and passing us on either side. About an hour outside of the city limits, however, the traffic thinned, and it became easier to relax and stare out the window. Villages dotted the landscape between stretches of open territory where zebras and ostriches roamed.

Eight hours later, the tarmac road ended. We drove a few kilometers on the dirt terrain and then pulled over.

"This is a "kiss" operation," Tano said. "The pick ups aren't equipped for the off-road conditions, so we will exchange cargo with the Land Cruiser that's coming from the base camp in northern Samburu."

When Tano said we'd "exchange" cargo, I didn't consider what that meant literally. But when the Land Cruiser arrived, it was full of Samburu patients who were being transported to Kenyatta Hospital.

The Samburu were tall, thin people with fine chiseled features, even more prominent because of their starvation. They wore hand crafted leather sandals and colorful cloths, wrapped around them almost like togas. The women were adorned with thousands of tiny colorful beads, bracelets that ran the length of their arms and necklaces that wrapped around and around their necks until even their collar bones were covered.

When the patients exchanged places with the cargo, I noticed that the Land Cruiser had a logo of a rifle with an X painted through it.

"What's the point of *that*?"

"To let bandits know that we are not armed."

"Bandits?"

"Don't worry," Tano said. "They know we are doctors. And we drive fast."

That was an understatement. For the next three hours we *flew* over deep, sandy ravines and crevassed dry river beds, reaching base camp just after nightfall. The team – a French doctor, a Dutch nutritionist, and a Spanish logistician - was waiting for us. We unloaded the gear by the light of the moon and the high beams of the Land Cruiser. Then we shared a small meal of bread and beans, pitched our tent, and Tano and I went to bed, snuggling under the sleeping bags that we had zipped together to make one.

Tano rose with the sun a few hours later.

"It's a beautiful morning," he said, leaning in the tent to hand me a cup of coffee.

"What time is it?" I asked sleepily.

"6 AM. I need to get started. There are already fifty children here. Come find me when you're dressed."

Drinking my coffee quickly, I looked for my pants. They were in a twisted heap at the feet of our sleeping bag, and as I pulled myself into them, I remembered the night, the passionate way we'd made love... and the fact that we'd whispered to each other for the first time about our desire to have a child. Natural impulsivity determined my next move, which was to skedaddle after him, birth control pill abandoned, thoughts of my very own baby jumbling together with my impatience to see the children in the feeding camp.

In daylight the landscape was breathtaking, hills of yellow and red earth stretching far into the distance under a magnificently deep blue sky.

The therapeutic feeding center – a makeshift bamboo structure with a tarp roof - was just a few meters from where we had slept. A thin figure approached from the distance, the shape of a child in her arms.

I took a few steps and realized something was not right.

My hands were lost in the pockets of my pants, the legs loose and baggy, bunching around my ankles.

I was wearing Tano's jeans.

Which meant that he was wearing mine.

I was six inches shorter than him and at least forty pounds lighter. How could he have even fit into my jeans?

Under the tarp, thirty women in colorful togas and the same intricate bead work I had seen on the road sat on red and black checkered blankets. Each was accompanied by at least one, sometimes two or three children, all of whom were emaciated.

Tano was examining a child whose feet and ankles were blown up like balloons.

"What is it?" I whispered.

"Kwashiorkor," he said, holding his stethoscope to the child's chest. Kwashiorkor was one manifestation of acute malnutrition, characterized by edema.

The mother did not take her eyes off of Tano's face as he gently turned her child on its side. Then he took a syringe from his pack, grasped the child's thigh in his hand – it was barely the size of my forearm - and injected something into the muscle.

The mother winced but the child remained listless.

He rubbed the little thigh and then moved to the next mother. She was holding a baby girl that looked like a skeleton.

Tano prepared another syringe.

"What is that?" I asked.

"The measles vaccination."

"*Measles?*"

"You don't see it in the West anymore because of good vaccination coverage," he said, injecting the small girl's leg. Like the child before him, she was too weak to even whimper. "But the germ is everywhere. It's the number one threat to these children's lives right now because their immune systems are so compromised. Just one case could provoke a disaster in the whole community."

When he'd finished his rounds we accompanied the team to the other feeding camps that had been erected around the territory. All day long Tano was oblivious to the fact that he was wearing my jeans, and I was struck by a tremendous feeling of love. He was so entirely unpretentious, walking around the feeding camps flashing a view of his tube socks right up to the elastic at his ankles.

We spent eight days in Samburu before starting the long journey back to Nairobi. I finally whispered the update of my skipped pills to Tano as we jolted across the desert, feeling thrilled when he said, "If you are pregnant, I will be so happy!"

Yet a few days later my period came.

Disappointed but not deterred, I stepped out of my dress as Tano walked through the door a week later.

"If at first you don't succeed…"

But for the first time since I'd gotten all ditzy, he spoke to me with a slight tone of reprimand.

"If you're serious about having a baby, *Querida*, I think you should get off the drugs."

His words were a buzz kill, even if I - who had done my therapy training in a drug treatment center! - knew he was absolutely right. Looking back through clinical eyes, I was clearly in some sort of drug-induced post traumatic mania. But having sunk so *low*, and having rebounded to what I believed to be a fabulous version of myself, I was actually afraid to do what I knew was the correct thing.

But common sense prevailed.

"OK," I conceded half an hour later, as I lay in the post coital position that Kavita had coached me in: behind propped up on a pillow, legs in the air, fingers crossed that sperm would meet egg.

And with that, I got off drugs -- recreational and psychopharmacologic. And since matters of mood were not what my husband was knowledgeable about, and since I was not being followed by any psychiatrist, we were unprepared for the plummet that followed.

The first signal that the chemicals were wearing off was the returned sense of dread about my job at USAID, even if the "new me" knew that whether I liked it or not, I should be grateful to have a source of income.

It was with that mind frame that I entered Phyllis's office one morning in early August, 1998, prepared to discuss my work plan. We had just sat down with fresh cups of coffee when BOOM!

The floor shook underneath us.

We gaped out the window as a billowing cloud of smoke rose over the city. Then an alarm sounded from within USAID, hollow and repetitive, followed by a voice blaring over the loudspeaker:

"THE AMERICAN EMBASSY HAS BEEN BOMBED. PEOPLE HAVE DIED. EVACUATE THE BUILDING IMMEDIATELY."

"Come," Phyllis cried, grabbing her purse and pulling me out of her office. We ran to the stairway, joining all of the people who were doing the same, people holding hands and looking bewildered. Some were crying and trying to call their spouses who worked at the Embassy.

By the time I got to the bottom of the stairs I had lost Phyllis. People were turning towards the parking lot while a security officer announced with a megaphone: "LEAVE THE PREMISES

IMMEDIATELY. DO NOT ATTEMPT TO GO TO THE EMBASSY. GO TO YOUR HOMES."

Outside the streets were full of Kenyans, looking dazed, walking away from downtown, towards Westlands.

"Madam!" a familiar voice shouted. It was Charles, prying open the passenger door with his crow bar.

I ran to him. "What is happening?"

"There was bomb at American Embassy," he said. "Let us pray to God for mercy. And now I will take you to your husband."

At MSF everyone stood in silence around the television in the meeting room, except Tano, who was in the radio room speaking to the Kenyan authorities.

The news reporter's voice was solemn.

"A bomb exploded in downtown Nairobi at 10:46 this morning. The situation is very dire. We need assistance."

The camera lingered on an enormous pile of rubble. People were climbing on it, trying to lift boulders, shouting for help.

Suddenly Tano strode into the room. "We've been called to Kenyatta Hospital. There are many shrapnel wounds and amputations. Let's go!"

The team was like a wave; they rose up and swelled out the door, fluid and unencumbered. I ran out behind them, my breath caught in my throat. I wanted to throw my arms around Tano, to cling to him, to share the grief I felt for poor, poor Nairobi, no longer my nemesis.

But he was already gone, speeding towards downtown with the team, where they would spend the next twelve hours in the blood soaked halls of Kenyatta Hospital.

By the next day we would know: The bombing had been politically motivated. It was Al Qaeda that had attempted to simultaneously blow up the US embassies in Dar es Salaam, the capital of Tanzania, and Nairobi. In Nairobi, over 5000 people were injured – many blinded or maimed for life - and 250 people dead. And though the US Embassy had been the target, of those killed, only twelve were American. The rest were Kenyans who had been going about their daily lives and who had died when the surrounding office buildings - unlike the heavily fortified Embassy – collapsed.

Like the aftershocks of an earthquake, the fallout of the bomb shook my fragile existence in Nairobi. Phyllis left on vacation a few days after the blast, but not before calling me with the news: because of heightened security, all non essential consultants would be cut from USAID's operations. I no longer had a job.

Swept along in the trauma that affected the city, my mood went from bad to worse, and I entered into a morose state that felt uncomfortable and disturbed.

Now, when Tano left for work in the morning, I remained in bed, drowsy and brooding.

"Since you're not working at all anymore," Tano said one day, "why don't you start baking again? I miss your cakes."

But the inspiration I'd found in baking was another victim of the bomb. Like the rubble heaped in the center of the city, my depression sat heavily in the center of my being.

"Just thinking of it makes me want to throw up."

"You exaggerate, *Querida*…"

But then I had to make a run for it. "Oh God…"

Tano stood outside the bathroom door. When I was done vomiting he came in. "You've been exhausted and now you're throwing up? When was your last period?"

I rinsed my mouth with water. "A few days after we got back from Samburu."

He did some quick mental math. "You haven't had a period for six weeks? Get dressed. We're going to the lab."

Tano wanted to wait to reveal my pregnancy, at least until I was three months along. But I just couldn't keep it to myself and announced the news immediately. It seemed to cheer everyone up, something to feel happy about in spite of the collective trauma of the bomb blast. Mama Florence, in particular, clucked around me, fluffing my pillows and scolding me for not eating correctly.

"Your baby is hungry, Madam," she'd say, each time she saw me press fresh carrots into juice.

Or "Madam, baby needs *food*," when she'd watch me slather peanut butter on whole wheat bread.

She wanted to feed me *ugali*. It was pure carbohydrate and had little nutritional value. But it filled the belly and was popularly considered "real" food. To make her happy, I grew accustomed to having several bowls a day.

Pregnancy infused me with a new sense of fortitude, as though the child growing inside would protect me from all violent crime with an invisible hormonal shield. Hence, after a few weeks of idly lying around (while Tano seemed to be slaving away more than ever), I decided that I should *do* something. And this is how I ended up in the back of Charles' taxi one afternoon, headed towards the offices of Childlife Trust, in downtown Nairobi.

Childlife Trust's main objective was to solicit and distribute donations to slum children. The Charity was housed in the storage space above the headquarters of a well-to-do paper products company called Kensta, whose managing director was a gorgeous Indian man called Anoop Shah. The Project Coordinator at the time was a young Kenyan woman named Rachel, who offered me *her* position ten minutes into our meeting.

"I've been accepted into a three months program at Nairobi University," she said eying my still small belly. "You could take over while I go to school."

It all felt a bit hasty, but why not? I shook her hand in agreement.

"Regarding donations, we never have enough to give to everyone that needs," she continued. "But if we have a *muzungu* working here, we will certainly receive more contributions from foreigners."

Now I understood why she wanted me, no questions asked. Widespread corruption had discouraged aid agencies from giving money to institutions like Childlife. With an expatriate involved, they might think there was less risk of abuse.

The ambiance at Childlife Trust was sometimes chaotic, an unmanageable number of idle volunteers hanging around the office, getting in the way of those who actually had something to do. Sometimes I didn't know who "worked" there and who was part of the steady stream of people coming through the doors all day long, looking for donations for their group.

The number of requests became overwhelming. We just didn't have that much inventory to distribute. Then it dawned on me that what we were lacking in material goods we could make up for with health education. I devoted my time to training the volunteers in basic counseling skills and the fundamentals of HIV prevention. For the first time since leaving the Teenage Clinic I felt truly useful.

I was lying on the sofa one evening, mulling over the work at Childlife Trust, and waiting for Tano to come home to run a few ideas by him. But when he came through the door, he had his own news to share. He'd been offered a job in Kampala, Uganda with Epicentre, MSF's Paris-based research satellite.

"Uganda?"

Uganda had recently been in all the headlines because a group of British and American tourists had been macheted to death in Bwindi National Park, along the Rwandese border.

"I'll be coordinating medical research programs in Uganda and South Sudan. Malaria and Sleeping Sickness. The job would be very interesting."

"Provided we haven't been massacred."

"Come on," he laughed. "Kampala is hours away from Bwindi. And it's a very safe city. Much safer than Nairobi."

I don't know why I acted so shocked. On my insistence we *had* agreed that after the baby was born, we'd leave Nairobi. But Uganda? I had been more in a New York state of mind.

"It would be an *easy* move," he said.

That felt like a shaky promise. But focused as I was on my expanding waistline, I had started to believe that really anything would be OK, as long as I had a healthy baby.

So I accepted.

By the eighth month of pregnancy, my bump was already huge and I was generally exhausted, unable to get comfortable at night between the heartburn and my constantly full bladder. I complained to Mama Florence, who said, "It is because you are very fat, Madam."

I tried not to glare. She had accompanied my belly expansion with a regular running commentary about how enormous I was.

"Really, *really* fat. Especially your face."

Although I understood that in Kenya it was considered good to be fat, especially during pregnancy – a sign that I had enough to eat – I was unable to hear these comments positively.

The next day Mama Florence came to work bearing a gift for me. It was a jar of earth.

"This is good for weak blood," she said. "You must eat it and you will feel better."

"Why, thank you Mama Florence," I replied, taken aback. I hoped she wasn't going to hand me a spoon next. "I'll have some later."

"Have much," she said. "Someone fat like you, Madam, you need much."

When she was outside washing clothes, I telephoned Tano.

"Geophagia," he said. "The practice of eating dirt."

"You know about this?"

"Many indigenous peoples do it. The earth contains minerals and iron that the pregnant body needs."

"You're not going to suggest that I--"

"No. Eating dirt can also give you parasites."

We got off the phone and I peeked out the window. Mama Florence was still washing. I scooped out several big spoonfuls of dirt and flushed them down the toilet. When she came in later I said, "I feel better already."

My due date came and went, and I began to feel desperate for labor to start. Epicentre wanted Tano in Uganda as soon as possible, and everyone had been counting on the baby arriving on time so that he could leave on schedule.

Mama Florence had some advice. "You must wake baby," she said, pointing at the stairs of our maisonette. "Run, but go *pole pole*."

Stair running did not produce the expected results, however, so she proposed another method.

"When you want to give birth and your baby is stubborn, you need to drive over bumpy roads. This works for Kenyan women."

At first Tano resisted, but when I threatened to take the car keys and give it a whirl myself, he agreed to drive – *pole pole* - in circles around our potholed compound. Even if we took the bumps gently, the car could not help but THA-THUNK over them, my big belly tha-thunking along with it.

I burst out laughing whenever we passed the guards. The first few rounds we made, they rose from their guard post to open the gate. We waved them away and continued our circular journey around the compound as they stared at us in bewilderment.

Tano got irritable as we made our fifteenth round. "This is ridiculous," he muttered. "If you want to get induced, let's do it properly at the hospital."

"Just shut up and drive," I giggled. "If you weren't in such a hurry to get to Kampala, I wouldn't be trying to speed the baby along anyway."

At 5 o'clock the following morning, I woke up feeling crampy. I lay there in the darkness, waiting for another contraction, hoping with all my might it would come.

When it did, ten minutes later, I shook Tano and whispered, "It worked! Wake up!"

"What?" he mumbled into the pillow.

"Mama Florence was right! I think labor is starting! I think the baby is coming!"

"Good," he said, sleepily, putting his arms around me. The clock said 5:18.

I went down to the kitchen and started to bake a cake. By 8:30 when Tano appeared, I had made not one, but two sponge cakes, the second of which was just coming out of the oven.

"How are the contractions?" he asked.

"About eight minutes apart. Can you go to *Uchumi* and get me some more eggs?"

Twelve hours – and one banana bread and a batch of carrot-zucchini muffins – later, my contractions were barely five minutes apart, and we left for Nairobi Hospital. I had gone through my pregnancy totally confident about this exact moment, knowing that it was going to hurt but determined to face the pain the way the Kenyan women did: with no epidural, no pain relief.

But I wasn't prepared for the midwife's comment after she examined me. "You're only two centimeters dilated. You've got a long night ahead of you."

"Why is it taking so long?" I wailed. I had thought we'd get to the hospital and I'd push the baby out.

"First babies are longer deliveries. You can help the process by staying on your feet. I know you are tired. I will ask the nurse to bring you some tea with sugar."

"Can I have milk in it?" I asked weakly.

"No milk," she said. "Just tea and sugar to give you energy." She turned to Tano. "Will you be here the whole time?"

"Yes, I was planning on staying."

"Fine," said the midwife, "But African men do not participate in birth. It is a woman's domain. The ward is full tonight, so keep to your wife's room so that the other laboring women don't feel uncomfortable."

After a night of intense suffering the midwife said, "*Now* you are ready to push."

"You can do it," Tano whispered in my ear, wiping the moisture from my face, a combination of sweat and tears.

"Now," she coached. "*Push.*"

I bore down as hard as I could, clenching my teeth and howling, once, twice and again until suddenly the pain dissipated, slithering out and erupting into fierce baby screams.

"It's a girl!" the midwife announced, putting the baby on my chest.

A *daughter*.

I cradled her bloody, rubbery little body in my arms, oblivious to everything but her adorable squished up face as the midwife snipped the umbilical cord. Then she took her from me to be weighed.

"Nine and a half pounds. Bravo!"

When the midwife brought her back, I read the nametag pinned on her uniform: *Makena*.

"What a pretty name," I said, woozy with happiness and hormones.

"It is Kikuyu," she replied. "It means joy."

"Makena," I said. "That's what I want to call my baby. *Makena.*"

"It is a good idea," she laughed. "A *muzungu* baby with a Kikuyu name."

I was completely in love.

Everyone had warned me about postpartum depression, but what I experienced was postpartum euphoria, utterly smitten with my baby, convinced that she was the smartest and most beautiful creature ever produced.

We returned to Westlands, four days after delivery. At home Mama Florence was waiting for us. She came whooping from the house as we pulled up.

"The Lord has blessed you!" she shouted, taking Makena from my arms. "You see, *ugali* made baby strong."

After Mama Florence left, we warmed some soup and ate quietly at the table while Makena slept, swaddled in a blanket on the sofa. We couldn't take our eyes off our new baby, and her precious presence filled all the space between us, so much so that we barely spoke of what was imminent: Tano's departure for Kampala.

The following morning a taxi came at 5:30 to take him to the airport. It was still dark outside and Makena did not stir from her nesting place between us as we shuffled out of the bedroom and down the stairs, the lock on the iron grille clanging when we opened it.

Tano held me tightly. "I'll come back for you as soon as I can."

Outside, the taxi honked. Abruptly he pressed his lips to mine. We stood like that for a long moment. Then he walked out of the house.

When he reached the car he turned back to look at me.

"I love you," he mouthed. *"Te amo."*

I closed the door and stood with my forehead pressed to the wood, listening to the chug of the old engine as the taxi bumped its way towards the front gate of the compound. The last three years of our life together flashed before me, from New Orleans to Nairobi.

In the bedroom, the first rays of the morning sun illuminated the bed in a soft yellow hue. Makena lay in the center of it, swathed in a faded pink blanket that had long ago been mine.

I lay down next to her, inhaling her fresh, new scent, listening to the rise and fall of her breath, imagining the life that lay ahead: a little girl becoming a woman.

Then I closed my eyes and exhaled.

UGANDA

Three weeks after his departure to Uganda, Tano came back for Makena and me. Upon arrival, he wanted to jump back in, literally and figuratively, to my life. But I was exhausted, having spent the last three weeks alone with a newborn. And fully engrossed in my love affair with Makena, Tano's presence felt somehow bothersome, an intrusion, and I resented having to hand *my* baby over to him, no matter how much I would have benefited from a break.

He was exhausted, too, he said, having spent his last weeks going around Uganda with his predecessor. It had been terrible for him, that handover time, leaving our brand new baby. And he'd missed *me*, he said. The weeks apart had made him realize how much he needed me.

But the newfound thrill with my very own love object had distanced me from Tano, and it was hard to feel empathetic. *He was always coming and going, and had never been very sympathetic about what that meant to me,* I thought. *So why should I feel sorry for him just because he'd been away for three weeks?*

This sentiment was compounded by the realization that while we had both just become parents for the first time, *my* life was the one that had *really* changed. So he'd been around Uganda and back... Big deal. He was still fully involved in his ever-the-more-interesting career...not to mention still sleeping soundly for at least seven hour stretches a night. Lived alone, Makena's noctural feedathons had felt like a thrilling maternal rite of passage. Now, blearily hoisting my voracious baby to my breast, Tano next to me, snoring away unfettered, my anger mounted. *How dare he snooze while I sit up all night with the baby?*

I seethed silently, my resentment stockpiling like so many hand grenades. Eventually the moment would arrive when I'd start throwing them. But for the moment, nothing was expressed. Instead, some invisible wall went up between us. And while the shift it created in our dynamic was subtle, it was undeniably there, and our relationship changed in the way our location changed, because while Uganda may have bordered Kenya to the West, it felt like an *entirely* different hemisphere.

Unlike the cool dry environment we had left behind, the air in Uganda was tropical, *heavy*, matching the mood that awaited us upon touchdown in the airport in Entebbe. The Epicentre driver, Elijah, was waiting for us in the arrivals halls. And he did not have good news.

"Doctor," he said, a somber expression on his face. "I could not get the drugs."

He was referring to the anti-malarials that Tano needed for the clinical trial he was launching in Mbarara, a southwestern town three hours from Kampala. The objective of the study was to find a new combination treatment because widespread drug resistance in Africa had rendered existing malaria treatments ineffective.

"Why, Elijah? What happened?"

"Bribe, Doctor. We need to give bribe."

The vein in Tano's temple throbbed, and he fell silent, moody and preoccupied as we made our way to Kampala on a two lane double direction road, where cars shared the turf with *matatus,* donkey carts, goats, chickens and pedestrians. Other than the ominous blue-black ocean of Lake Victoria, everything around us was otherwise *green*: lush foliage grew thickly, interspersed with palms and *matoke* - *ma-to-kay* – a type of plaintain that was the Ugandan equivalent to *ugali*. As we approached the city, stalls heaped with fruits and vegetables dotted the roadside, colorful signs of life that contrasted starkly with the other industry that was apparently booming: simple pine caskets, many intended for children and babies, underlying the omnipresence of AIDS.

Kampala was small compared to Nairobi. The few tall buildings dwarfed the shanty town sprawl, and the scene outside the window was vibrant. Men and women were dressed in traditional garb, and many carried large bundles on their heads: trays of oranges and mangos, stacks of plastic buckets, a tower of bicycle tires.

We got settled in a middle class neighborhood called Kansanga, in a house that doubled as the Epicentre office and guesthouse. Surrounded by an immense iron fence, the house was also rigged with a sophisticated security system complete with panic buttons, double barring on the windows, a steel door separating the bedroom area from the rest of the house, *and* an armed guard. While this did not engender the idea that "Kampala was much safer than Nairobi," as Tano had claimed, I *loved* all the protection, especially since the magic hormonal shield of my pregnancy had more or less dissipated now that I had my chubby babe in arms. And I adored the house itself, a sprawling one story African style rancher, light and airy, looking out over a beautiful garden and in the distance, Ggaba Hills.

Each day, crowing roosters woke us at dawn. Days ended early too, since the electricity died every other night at 7 PM sharp, and stayed off until 10 PM, the government's way of preserving energy.

Nights Makena and I went to bed early, sometimes as soon as the power went off, while Tano stayed up late, furiously working on the protocol for the malaria trial. Although he spoke passionately about the study, getting it off the ground presented innumerable logistical problems, and I gave up trying to follow after those first weeks in Uganda. Sometimes this didn't work, sometimes that didn't work, and everything that went wrong impacted the smooth functioning of something else. Tano spent his days either closed in his office, or going back and forth between Kampala and Mbarara, trying to accomplish objectives that rarely, if ever, were attainable without a very stressful and upsetting series of hitches that set him back by another day, week, or month.

My days, on the other hand, were spent with my neighbor, another MSF wife, a gorgeous *Parisienne* redhead named Nicole, who was five months pregnant with her first baby. We took to each other the way dye takes to water, and spent hours together those first months in Uganda, *solidaire* in our new maternal states, our marriages to MSF cowboys, and my latest *topic du jour*: Mabel.

Mabel was the housekeeper who "came" with the house, a system that I loathed in spite of the protracted friendship I'd shared with Mama Florence. Yet unlike Mama Florence and her cheerful, benevolent presence, Mabel gave me the creeps, with her peculiar wild eyed appearance and a strange odor emanating from her skin.

Elijah, the driver, clued me in one day while teaching me how to drive the second hand stick shift that Tano had purchased for me. I had just lurched us out onto the dusty back roads of Kansanga when he said, "Madam. I want to give you warning. Mabel, she drinks *waragi*."

Waragi was distilled alcohol – moonshine, really – and from what I'd heard, dangerously toxic. So *that* was the smell --pungent, somehow like ethanol.

"And she does bad witchcraft, Madam."

Witchcraft!

At first I went to Tano.

"That's nonsense," he said, when I repeated Elijah's warning. "Surely you don't believe in witchcraft?"

I didn't reply. It was hard to discount totally the deep belief of almost every Kenyan I'd met – and it appeared the Ugandans felt the same. And if anyone fit my stereotype of a witch, it was Mabel.

"I just wish he'd *fire* her," I complained to Nicole.

Her reply was the obvious one: *tell* him that. Or fire her yourself.

But what I couldn't even tell my new best friend was that my aversion to Mabel had metastasized into a fear of her. With that came the belief that if fired, she would seek revenge by doing something to me, or the thing I loved most in the world: Makena.

"Oh I've told him!" I complained, launching into my newest version of *isn't my husband a jerk?* "I've told him and he won't do anything about it."

At home the conversations actually went more like this:

"Tano, I think Mabel might really be a witch."

"That's crazy."

"Elijah is scared of her, too."

"I suppose you want me to fire her?"

"No! I mean, I want you to if *you* want to."

"Well *I* don't want to."

"Really?"

"What are we talking about, *Querida*?"

And I'd slink away, frustrated that I couldn't find a way to get Tano to fire her of his own free inspiration, which in my mind was the only safe way for her to go. (For the record, since Tano didn't believe in voodoo, I just assumed he *couldn't* get bumped off).

In the midst of the mounting tension over Mabel, and all the setbacks with the malaria trial, Pia arrived. A young Finnish woman recruited by the Paris office, Pia had been hired as the field coordinator for the Mbarara study. Having never set foot in Africa, however, she touched down in Uganda and promptly spiraled into a state of almost unmanageable anxiety – especially when she discovered that her lodging was an isolated house on the outskirts of Mbarara.

Tano's solution was to keep her in Kampala with us, or stay with her in Mbarara so she wouldn't be alone. At least until he could find her a new house. I should have been more sympathetic to her plight – Lord knew I could relate to her panic – but it annoyed me that we were once again living with the team. And the mirror she presented provoked another type of discomfort, for every time she bemoaned the insecurity she felt, it reminded me of my own sense of inadequacy that I was not able to just breeze past the idea of carjackers and bandits as though they were mere inconveniences.

"Could they be having an affair?" Nicole speculated one afternoon as we sipped tea on the patio.

"No!"

I replied with such vehemence that Nicole threw up her hands in mock defense. Aside from the fact that Pia was not the type to mess with someone else's husband, she was so much like *me*, with her long list of neuroses, how could Tano possibly be attracted to her?

Yet Nicole's suggestion clearly gave me pause, because thereafter I began analyzing every little move – what Tano said, or didn't, how he looked at me, or didn't, and I even found myself lingering behind doorways whenever Pia was around, trying to detect if there wasn't some hidden exchange in their endless discussions of mosquito larva, prophylaxis, and the politics of it all.

One morning I found him sitting on the patio, a steaming mug of coffee in his hand, staring out into the distance. He and Pia had had another late night in front of the computer and he looked rumpled, tired, but when I stepped out onto the patio with Makena, his expression lifted. I took the cue and went to him, pouring Makena, now three months old, into his lap and rubbing his shoulders, a spontaneous and now rare act of affection.

"Thank you," he sighed. "That feels good."

"What were you thinking about?"

"Nothing. Everything." He yawned. "The study."

We stood in silence, save for the birds performing a symphony in the garden. It could have been a perfect moment. But then it slipped out.

"Are you attracted to Pia?"

"Now I know you are really *loca*," he said, shaking my hands off his shoulders.

I regretted my words instantly. But instead of dropping it, I had to make it worse. "I just ask because she's so *scientific*."

Tano stared straight ahead, his jaw fixed in a firm line of irritated impatience.

"And she's *Finnish*. It's much more politically correct than being Ameri--"

"Get a job. *Please*."

"What does that have to do with anything?" I snapped, trying to snatch Makena back from him, but she started to wail so I had to let go.

"You have way too much free time. And you spend it thinking about witches and affairs."

"I'm a mother now."

"That's beside the point. You *need* to work. You're miserable when you don't. And then you make me miserable."

I was about to revert to my old Nairobi litany – *I don't have a stable career because I followed you!* – but when I heard Pia's footsteps approaching the patio, I fled to the kitchen instead, filled with embarrassment for the stupid way I'd just acted. Why was I trying to pick a fight? And why was I so defensive? Tano's comment stung, but if I was going to be honest with myself, he was absolutely right: I *did* need a job. I *wanted* a job - as badly as ever. Motherhood had not killed my desire for career. I just hadn't really considered how to operationalize my next move.

I poured myself some coffee and took a swig, but it was scalding and burned and I spit the bitter mouthful into the sink. I made a new pot and as it hissed and dripped, I resolved that I would apologize to Tano for my mercurial behavior...and tell him that I would start a job search. Soon. I just needed to figure out how to be Mommy *and* career woman...and could we talk about this together? There were so many things I wanted to talk to him about.

When the coffee was ready I poured us both a mug, and moved swiftly back through the house, prepared to make my little speech.

But when I got to the patio there was Pia, buttering her toast, nodding seriously at whatever Tano was saying, something about double-blind control groups.

A few weeks later, I held Makena in my arms and looked down with a sense of dizzy astonishment at the crisp angles of Washington, DC tilting below me as the 747 banked to land. It was a bright fall day, the sun beating down on the roofs of the sleek cars cruising in perfect order along unblemished black highways, a complete contrast to the chaos and lack of uniformity that was Africa.

I had avoided returning to the US until now. The carjacking, the bomb blast and all the other stressors had morphed into a belief that the long flight would likely end in fiery catastrophe. But both our families now waited desperately to meet Makena – she was the first grandchild on both sides – so I decided to take my chances. She and I were to spend one month in Washington and then meet Tano in Argentina for another month.

As expected, my parents were overjoyed with their granddaughter. But my family's thrill with the baby and their wistfulness that we lived so far away was soon swallowed up by the announcement that MSF had won the Nobel Prize.

The Nobel Prize!

I sat with my parents in the TV room listening to the news report, illustrated with footage of disaster and despair from around the world. My parents expressed their admiration openly, reveling in the vicarious sense of meaning and purpose that we all gleaned from our insider connection to the organization.

By the time we touched down in Argentina, Tano was a celebrity, and I a celebrity wife. But as all the local newspapers and TV stations in his province did stories on us, a begrudging sense of rivalry mounted.

"Qué privilegio estar casada con él," a young woman in the grocery store said to me one evening, recognizing us from one of the newspaper articles. *What a privilege to be married to him.*

I smiled graciously, but privately my thoughts seethed: *I just had a baby, you know! And then I was ALONE, in Nairobi with a newborn for almost a MONTH! And now I have to put up with a drunken witchdoctor!*

The more compliments that came my way, about how lucky I was to have Tano, the more any grievance —legitimate or not – that had ever crossed my mind was added to my stockpile of explosive emotional devices, and I sat perched, waiting for *any* opportunity to lob one at him.

Yet no matter how many I lobbed, he refused to blow up, not even when I meanly told him I thought marriage was overrated, about fifteen minutes before he was to accept the keys to his city, a ceremony organized by the mayor in honor of MSF. Although a look of utter hurt colored his expression, he said *nothing*, which only spurred me to rant and rave harder, trying to get some reaction.

In spite of my crazed private attacks on Tano, I was evolved enough to keep it together in the presence of my lovely family in law. So in the weeks we were there, I chatted and smiled amiably over countless *asados* and other family gatherings. Meanwhile my thoughts were preoccupied with the only thing anymore on my personal TO DO list:

GET A JOB.

I'd been scouring the international job pages since Tano's commentary a couple months back, but so far nothing that I could imagine doing had presented itself. Then, a few days before we were to return to East Africa, I saw it:

Project Director - Uganda.

My eyes flew over the text. A Minnesota based NGO needed a Project Director, preferably with a background in public health. The NGO, which was in a rural district of southwest Uganda called Ssembabule, three hours by road from Kampala, had two main objectives: to combat widespread Vitamin A deficiency by promoting community gardens, and to provide HIV/AIDS counseling services. Applicants were to email their CVs. A phone number was listed. I scribbled it down and raced to the phone.

It was that easy. One phone call, central Argentina to central United States. One brief conversation, job still available, please meet outgoing director immediately upon return to Uganda.

We stopped in Paris on our way back to Kampala. Tano's colleague, Frédéric, left on mission, leaving us the keys to his apartment, which epitomized a Parisian garret: a dollhouse size bathroom and a tiny kitchen, two small bedrooms with oak floors and marble fireplaces, an elegant little living room that gave to the wonderful rooftops of the 11th *arrondissement*.

Oh, Paris!

I was in heaven.

While Tano attended meetings at Epicentre, I hung out with Nicole, who took up residency for a few nights in the second bedroom with her new baby boy, Pierre, born in Paris six weeks earlier.

As we lounged on the sofa together, breastfeeding our babies, I had a slight twinge of guilt: *Was I a bad mother? Was it wrong to try to return to the workforce while Makena was so little?*

But talking it through with Nicole reassured me. *"C'est normale,"* she said. *"Many* French mothers work. And if working makes you happy, then *it's obligatoire*...You must find a job. Because if you are not happy, your child is going to be unhappy, too. Children *know."*

The day after we got back to Kampala, I met the outgoing director of Minnesota International Health Volunteers, Zoa Foguel, at the Speke Hotel in downtown Kampala, where a bomb had exploded, just a year earlier. Traces of the explosion were still visible in one corner of the restaurant, where charred wood in the wall had not been completely repainted.

"It was planted by a militant Islamist group," explained Zoa, whose pony-tailed, cheerful appearance evoked some past life as a camp counselor. But unlike a camp counselor, her enthusiasm was less pep than *intensity*: she ate and breathed the Ssembabule project in the same way Tano lived his work. It was not her job. It was her calling.

I watched her mouth move as she spoke, a torrent of words floating around my ears and putting me into a sort of trance.

"We've been promoting community gardens for so long, the program is almost running itself...Do you have any experience gardening?"

I didn't, but I wanted the job badly enough to lie, figuring I could get Tano to show me how to work a hoe and shovel. *I imagined us in the garden together, wearing overalls and planting potatoes...*

Zoa and I spent several hours together, and what I lacked in knowledge about Vitamin A, I was able to make up for in discussing HIV and counseling techniques. Visibly impressed, Zoa decided then and there that I fit the part, and offered me the job.

That night Tano pulled out a bottle of champagne that he'd carried back from France for a special occasion.

"I think this counts, no?" he said, corking the bottle.

I felt an instant jolt of guilt for all the negativity I'd projected at him since Makena's birth. Her sleeping patterns had recently normalized, and I was no longer feeling so exhausted. This fact alone made me warm back up to Tano, and it suddenly occurred to me how nice it actually was to be together, drinking champagne in our fortress in Kampala, Uganda, precious baby sleeping in the next room, both of us with our evolving careers. But in spite of this good cheer, we drank the champagne in silence, and went to bed, each one of us to our own side, no touching at all -- not even our toes – already too far out of the habit of snuggling up to know how to move back towards the middle.

Zoa called the very next day to finalize the contract, which we faxed back to Minnesota, my signature scrawled boldly across the bottom of the page. A few days later, she and I traveled to Ssembabule together, Makena in tow.

The route was verdant, flourishing, winding through forest in some parts and open plains in others, past Lake Victoria, where leafy fields of papyrus grew, their plume-like stalks swaying as though greeting us hello and goodbye. But a maudlin feeling crept in just before we turned off the tarmac onto the dirt road that would carry us another fifty kilometers into rural Ssembabule, when we happened upon the burning carcass of an oil truck. It had overturned – probably speeding – and a crowd had gathered to loot it. The looters were siphoning oil from the trucks' tank when someone came along with a cigarette and the whole thing blew.

Charred corpses were lined up on the roadside, at least one of which was female, the baby on her back burned beyond recognition.

"Desperation," Zoa said.

"It's awful," I murmured, unable to tear my eyes from the macabre scene. I watched the smoke curl above the bodies until the matoke grew so thick my view was obscured.

Arriving, finally, at the project site, I expected to find a scene from Tano's world: people desperately ill or dying. But instead we pulled up at what looked like a little farmstead, a simple concrete structure in the middle of a field, the terrain around it overrun with goats and chickens. Zoa honked as we approached, and the animals scattered, squawking and *beeeehing* as if to protest our arrival.

Fifty meters behind the office was a modest three bedroom house where Zoa had been living for the past five years, a fact that I had either not understood or been in total denial about, because it seemed that she thought I was going to be doing the same.

"It's a great place to raise kids," she said, gesturing to the open land. "You'll see."

"Oh sure," I replied, vaguely, as Makena happily flapped her arms at the goats and chickens.

It became quickly apparent that Zoa was going to be a tough act to follow. She was a dynamo: smart, savvy, and totally at ease in this rural African scene. And while she went on and on about the women's empowerment groups and the district's Vitamin A deficiency and polio immunization campaign, my mind was distracted by a few other realities about Ssembabule that had emerged: no electricity, no phone service, and – horror! – not even a lock on the door of the house I was supposed to live in.

By the time we retired to the house that evening, I was mentally exhausted. Zoa had charged through hundreds of talk points, referring to many things in acronym, some public health code that only the Zoas and Tanos of the world knew.

Night fell, a black blanket of sky, illuminated only by the moon and the fire that someone – *a guard?* – had started outside and upon which Zoa prepared us a simple dinner. As she cooked, she continued to speak about the project, and I continued to nod and ask questions, determined to make this work in spite of the doubts that had been swelling inside me all day long.

I could learn all those public health codes, I rationalized (*Thank God for Tano*)... and I supposed even my (now raging) anxiety disorder could be managed: *I could get a lock installed on the door, a shortwave radio, a prescription for valium?*

Then came the reverie-shattering pronouncement:

"Every single one of us has had a very difficult time coping with the murder."

"*MURDER?*"

"I didn't tell you?" Zoa sounded genuinely confused. "Cecie. She worked at headquarters in Minnesota. She was a dear friend and colleague." Her voice broke. "She was only thirty four years old."

Adrenaline surged through my body. "What *happened*?"

"It was right before the Nairobi bomb blast....Maybe two weeks?" She blew her nose noisily. "She had come to Uganda for a field visit."

"And she was killed in *Ssembabule?*"

"No. Kampala. In a hotel. Someone came to her room, posing as a maintenance man. He stabbed her to death."

My *God*.

I felt instantly hysterical. I wanted to run, as fast and as far as I could, from Ssembabule, from East Africa, from my life. *For* my life.

"*Everyone* loved Cecie," Zoa said. "Everyone. She was one of those people that was genuinely good – she didn't have a mean bone in her body."

"Did they catch the guy?"

"He turned himself in. He was a serial killer, someone crazy. He confessed to the crime."

After a while the conversation moved back to more banal topics, like abject poverty and scurvy, and then we called it a day. But sleep did not come, intoxicated as I was with anxiety, clinging to my sleeping daughter as images of serial killers drilled through my head like a jackhammer.

How on earth was I going to deal with this job?

All night I *yearned* for Tano, craved his calm rationality, his sensible, measured way of moving through the world. What would he say right now? I tried to channel his epidemiologist's brain: What *was* the probability of two people from the same agency getting murdered? But 50-50 was all I could come up with: It would either happen again, or it wouldn't.

By sun up I had decided I had to just tell Zoa: I wasn't the right person for the job. It felt embarrassingly selfish to withdraw now, not to mention a complete and total admission of defeat. I thought of how badly I wanted to work. And I thought of Cecie Goetz. Who knew what apprehensions she might have had in her life, but at least she had been making an effort in spite of it.

Yet whatever resolve I'd had to quit was swept to the wayside by what followed.

A knock sounded at the door. A man with the physical build of an ox stood in the entryway.

"We have come to say goodbye to Madam Zoa." His manner was gentle as he gestured to the small group standing behind him. "And to meet you, Madam. We are the SACS counselors."

SACS stood for Ssembabule AIDS Counseling Services, and Sunday was the leader of the group of nine, all of them farmers. After the introductions had been made, leaving no time for my lame resignation, Zoa sent me off with the counselors on a tour of the district.

Over several hours we visited one bleak homestead after another. If the people we met were not sick themselves, they were caring for infirm relatives, or those that the dead had left behind. One toothless grandmother, her face wrinkled like a dried fruit, had eleven children in her charge. The eldest – ten and eleven years old – helped her work the land. But it had been a hard year.

"They struggle, Madam," said Sunday. "Life in the village is very difficult."

His comment was such an understatement that all I could do was nod dumbly in agreement.

"We thank God when there is rain," he added. "Because then we have good crops. But last year the rain did not come. We were all hungry for many months. We suffered, Madam."

He looked at me expectantly, as though I might have some insight to offer, but all I could manage was to nod again, patently aware that I had no idea at all what that really meant.

Back in Kampala that evening, I lay on the sofa, my arm thrown dramatically across my eyes, as Tano lectured me on the probabilities of a second MIHV staff person being murdered.

"Nil, *Querida*. Really. Especially if the crime was committed by a serial killer who is now in jail."

Although that "detail" bothered me too. How many serial killers did one actually hear of in Africa?

"You can do this," Tano encouraged me. "It's a chance for you to *really* work, to learn new things."

I groaned.

"Think of Pia. She's doing very well now."

This was true. After a few shaky months (and moving into a less isolated house), Pia had come into her own and was now confidently holding down the fort in Mbarara.

"But Pia has *you*."

"You have me, too," Tano replied. "I'll help you in any way I can. I just want to see you accomplish your goals."

And to think I'd accused him of being unsupportive…

That night I wiggled over to his side of the bed, trying to envelope him in a full body embrace. "I know I've been hard to live with, Tano. I'm sorry."

But his arms remained stiffly at his sides.

"Darling?" I whispered, teasingly. But when he didn't turn towards me, not even a centimeter, I propped myself up on my elbow. "Is everything alright?"

"You think marriage is overrated."

Images of my petulant proclamation in Argentina flooded my mind, and I felt like a total heel. But instead of telling him that, I argued that after everything we'd been through, I had the "right" to be resentful. After all, our time in East Africa had not been easy. Not for me, anyway.

"Do not blame me for your problems, *Querida*," he said. "Now you have a chance for a real job and you're already thinking of quitting. You are a very complicated woman."

His tone indicated that this was absolutely not intended as a compliment, and my face smarted in the dark. *It's not me that's complicated*, I wanted to protest…

Or was it?

But I didn't say anything, finally, because Tano's breathing had already evened. Just like that, he was asleep, leaving me alone to toss and turn all night long. By morning, however, some combination of his pep talk, his castigation, and my desire to work with the SACS counselors won out over my trepidation.

And that was how I found myself toodling off to Ssembabule every week thereafter. I hired a babysitter to help me with Makena, a young woman named Rose who actually hailed from Ssembabule… and ironically, walked with a crutch, having been crippled by polio as a child. Although I eventually got accustomed to leaving Makena in Kampala with her, the three of us would often travel to the field together.

Thereafter, I managed to contain my concerns, at least enough to do the job. Of course, I made some adjustments to the way Zoa had done things. First I had a lock installed on the door. But after a couple of sleepless overnights nonetheless, I made the executive decision to either go back and forth from Kampala in the day, or to stay in a little hotel in Masaka, the last town before we turned onto the dirt road to Ssembabule. If it's any indicator of how bad my mental health really was, the nights I stayed in the hotel, I carried rope in my suitcase, so that I could loop an elaborate lock system on the windows and doors. Makena thought it was a game, and Rose certainly thought I was completely nuts, but I sucked up my pride and proceeded with my roping ritual. I just wasn't able to sleep otherwise, outside of the high security confines of our house in Kampala.

It's as though I had two lives, in two competing worlds: the inner one in which I lived -- a dangerous, unforgiving place, filled with carjackers, bandits, and now, serial killers, too; and the outer one, in which I moved -- a colorful, musical, vibrant Africa full of interest and possibility.

To this day I try to imagine how my years in East Africa would have evolved if we had not been carjacked. Or how things might have played out differently if I had received appropriate mental health care in its aftermath. Because in reality, I had become as crippled as my babysitter, struggling every day to balance my two worlds, trying to keep the inner one under control so that I could proceed with the duties required of me on the outside, where my days were now filled with a new routine of vaccinations, Vitamin A, and HIV counseling.

As Zoa had promised, some of the programs were so integrated that they almost ran themselves. The work with the SACS counselors, however, was a process of reinvention, born in response to their discouragement that in this destitute context, traditional "counseling" was hardly a useful service.

Sunday, the only counselor who spoke both Luganda and English fluently, had translated the counselor's claims:

Counseling is not enough. When there is no food and no doctor, it does not matter what we feel about it.

Adults are living in isolation with too many orphans to care for.

Adults are weakened by the disease, cannot keep up with their farm work, and they lose their crops.

Without crops to sell and earn money, parents can no longer afford their children's school fees.

Traditional practices are spreading the disease.

Comments about traditional practices brought to mind all the misinformation I'd heard at the Teenage Clinic in Nairobi. And so I asked Sunday, "Which practices?"

"You have heard of wife inheritance?"

"Yes," I nodded. The practice was the same in Kenya. When a woman's husband died, his brother inherited the widow.

"This spreads AIDS. Another problem is the old men who seduce young girls with promises, to pay their school fees, or provide them a daily meal."

Sugar Daddies. They were everywhere.

"And there are still other beliefs that cause people to play sex even if their partner might be infected."

"Play sex?"

"Yes. If they don't play, the males think the penis will become small, like a bean."

I laughed. But his expression was somber.

"The females, they believe the vagina will harden. Like wood. Then it will not work for producing children. So you see. Our people must play sex."

I'll have to research this, I thought as I sped back towards Kampala that evening, a bizarre array of images dancing through my head.

Vaginas turning to wood?

Penises turning to beans?

I wondered what kind of bean he had meant – string bean or kidney?

After months of discussion and research, we revamped the SACS counseling program into a series of therapeutic and educational retreats for families affected by AIDS.

The retreats were planned to take place in three day cycles, and would include discussion of cultural practices that spread disease, and growing and using vegetables and herbs with known palliative properties to treat AIDS related syndromes and boost nutrition. Time would also be spent on developing community "survival strategies," such as helping villagers better share the burden of caring for orphans and the elderly, as well as dividing farm labor amongst the healthy to increase food production for all. I also incorporated a basic stretching routine into the curriculum, so that caregivers could learn techniques to keep the muscles of the bedridden active.

When I presented this idea to the counselors, showing them chosen postures from a yoga manual, I assumed that their laughter was because I looked so ridiculous demonstrating neck rolls, toe touches and waist bends. It was when Sunday flipped to the diagrams of advanced postures, recommended only for the most experienced yogis, that I realized the real source of their amusement: I had totally overlooked their physical prowess. They studied the pictures for a few seconds, and then casually performed "Crow," and then "Scorpion," and then, as I stood there gaping, threw themselves into headstands. I couldn't believe it, although I shouldn't have been so astonished, given that these men had been working the fields their whole lives and had bodies of rock solid muscle -- and minds of pure determination.

Motivated by the counselor's dedication and the outpouring of interest from the Ssembabule community, headquarters in Minnesota applied for – and was awarded – a 20,000 dollar grant from the Conservation, Food and Health Foundation in Boston. This money, a fortune in rural Africa, would fund our retreats for an entire year.

The day I learned we'd been awarded the money, however, I celebrated alone. I couldn't call the Ssembabule office because there was no phone service, and Tano was far away, also out of reach of any simple telecommunications, in an area of Northern Uganda called Omugo, where MSF ran a sleeping sickness treatment center. He had already been away for a week, and from there would travel by road to Ibba, a village in South Sudan where there was another MSF treatment center.

Sleeping sickness – or Human African Trypanasomiasis- was spread by the bite of the tse tse fly, who injected a parasite into the victim's blood. The first stage of the disease resembled a more common flu, but in later stages, as the parasite invaded the brain, the infected person would literally go insane before falling into a coma and dying.

A drug by the name of Eflornithine, originally developed by pharmaceutical companies as a potential treatment for cancer, had proven to be miraculously effective in treating sleeping sickness. When it proved to be ineffective as an anti-cancer, however, its production was stopped.

MSF had the last 1000 doses in stock in the whole world. Of the hundreds of thousands of people in central Africa infected by sleeping sickness, only a few thousand received treatment. And most of them, because of the dearth of Eflornithine, were given the only other known treatment – Melarsoprol - a derivative of arsenic that was corrosive to the veins. That this treatment killed about 6% of patients who received it was the reason that Epicentre, under Tano's leadership, was launching a clinical trial to find a new treatment protocol.

The trip from Kampala to Omugo was just an hour and half by plane, but from Omugo to Ibba it was fourteen hours by car, a journey complicated not only by the extremely rough roads but by the presence of the SPLA – the Sudan People's Liberation Army – a rebel army who patrolled the region and suspected anyone affiliated with France or a French organization of being a spy.

Between my journeys to and from Ssembabule, and his between Kampala, Mbarara, Omugo and Ibba, Tano and I now saw each other almost only in passing. He would arrive and I would be leaving, so we'd have quick check-ins about household matters (Mabel) and our adored daughter. At one moment I had tried to revisit my hurtful statement about marriage, but Tano told me that he preferred to not discuss it any further.

"But how do you *feel*?" I had insisted.

"That's my private business."

"Tano, we're married. We're *supposed* to talk these things through."

But silence was his preferred method for facing painful sentiments, and it was a *modus operandi* for which I had no adequate defense. Hence, old hurts that lingered, or new ones that got churned up, were neatly packaged into our mutual avoidance of talking anymore about our relationship. And then, as if it were a natural marital segue, the time we did manage to spend together took on a collegial tone.

"This cannot be good," Nicole warned one evening as we caught up over a glass of wine.

"I just don't know how to bridge the distance," I told her woefully, although this was only a half truth. What I did not reveal to her was that Tano had apparently recovered from his hurt enough to recently launch a few advances in my direction.

"Let's go to Murchison Falls for the weekend, *Querida*. Or plan a trip to Bwindi," he had proposed on more than one occasion.

These propositions had been accompanied with some physical gesture of a long forgotten intimacy: a kiss on the nape of my neck, a hand placed intentionally on the small of my back.

But what I couldn't tell my rational husband anymore than I cared to admit to my best friend, was that in spite of my progress as a professional, zipping off to Ssembabule almost every week, I was still far too terrified to go to *these* places – the tourist hot spots that people in the West would spend *thousands* to get to. Here, too, I'd worked out my own form of witchcraft, of the obsessional type: That if I just stuck to a certain routine and never deviated from it, no harm would come to me - or my daughter.

And so, Tano and I went nowhere together.

But I always came up with "reasonable" excuses for my relational lethargy: usually some variation on not being able to get away because I had too much work. The avoidance of any personal outing with my husband was compounded by the fact that Nicole and Loic were soon leaving Uganda for good, and had therefore begun to take *every* weekend away, visiting all the places that I refused to consider.

"You really have no desire at all to see something of Uganda other than Kampala and Ssembabule?" Tano asked one evening. "I saw Loic and he invited us to climb Mount Elgon with him next month."

But I invented another excuse, and that was the last time I can recall Tano extending an invitation to me while still on African soil.

Unfortunately, by the time the Mount Elgon weekend arrived, a real, tragic excuse had evolved. One of the MIHV staff people, a young woman named Eva Nakalema, had been killed when the matatu she was traveling in blew a tire and flipped multiple times on the road to Ssembabule. The entire team was traumatized, and we helped her family organize for the funeral, including picking up her body at the morgue.

The funeral was an all day, heart wrenching experience, in the middle of which I was asked, as the Director of MIHV, to make a speech. I felt anything but directorly, faced with Eva's family's raw anguish, and my mind was flooded with catastrophic images: *matatu* wreck victims splayed on the road to Ssembabule, myself shot in the head by the carjackers, Tano shot in the back by the SPLA, Cecie struggling at the hands of the serial killer...

Life and death, life and death...

Life.

Death.

I wanted to scream and cry with Eva's family.

Instead, I made the speech.

Home from the funeral that evening, I lay on the bed, exhausted, mindlessly thumbing through Tano's encyclopedia of tropical medicine, a thick volume filled with photos of necrotic wounds, scaly intestinal worms, and testicles that had blown up twenty times their normal size with elephantiasis. But when I heard his car pull into the compound, I shoved the book aside and ran out to the driveway to greet him.

"I thought you weren't coming back until tomorrow!"

"We climbed fast," he said, kissing me lightly on the cheek. "And an old friend was on the climb. He's going to stay with us for a few days." He gestured to the car. "He says you already know each other."

"Ca fait plaisir de te revoir," a tall man with a thick mop of salt and pepper hair climbed from the passenger seat. "Do you remember me?" He leaned towards me to do the *bise*. "Jacques Rivière."

It took just one disorienting second before it all flooded back: *The goodbye dinner. Nairobbery. Jacques.*

Handsome, perceptive, sympathetic Jacques, who had diagnosed my "weakness" with barely a glance. How strange the mind was: I hadn't thought about him since that night almost two years earlier, but now, standing here in the twilight, I was filled with a retroactive sense of attraction. He was *gorgeous*!

That night the three of us had dinner on the patio. They told me about the climb, and I told them all about the funeral and how shaken I'd been by the family's grief.

"When I worked in Burundi I attended a couple of those a *day*," Jacques said.

The three of us polished off a bottle of Bordeaux as we talked and I learned that Jacques was forty years old and had spent the last fifteen years in the field with MSF as a logistics coordinator. He was French, from Marseille, but worked with MSF Holland, who had loaned him to MSF - France to assist with the sleeping sickness trial.

We had just corked another bottle when Tano excused himself to catch up on some emails. Jacques and I stayed on the patio talking, and then he tailed me through my household duties, helping me clear the table and clean up the kitchen.

"So," I heard myself saying as the sink filled with soapy water, "Never been married?"

"No. Commitment phobic, I guess." He started gently sliding plates into the suds. "And I haven't found a woman that can deal with all my travel."

For some reason his comment made me laugh.

"It's not hard? Always having Tano away? And with a little one?"

Was this man hand delivered by the empathy God?

"We manage," I said offhandedly. "It's not that bad." Then I surprised myself. "But I suppose we've become a little bit immune to each other."

"Immune to you?" Jacques laughed, in a way that was clearly meant to flatter. "Impossible."

I smiled and scrubbed the plates. But inside I was realizing: *That* was it. Somewhere along the way, Tano and I had stopped really *feeling* each other. We were co-parents. Colleagues. Even friends – sort of. Always cordial, now. Agonizingly so. Because some deeper malaise had infiltrated our bond. And I only just realized it because this evening with Jacques Rivière had activated some *energy*, so tingly and delicious, that if he had suddenly said, "Hey, lets go to Bwindi," I would have replied, "What time do we leave?"

For the next few days I tried to focus on my work: I had another round of counseling retreats to plan for, and I also had to write a report for our donors detailing how we used the first chunk of grant money. But it was hard to get back to business as usual after Eva's funeral. And if that sad event had infused me with yet another jolting dose of mortality, Jacque's presence had injected me with its antidote: a sexy, coursing sense of vitality. I tried to steer clear of him, but he sought me out - ostensibly to help with the dishes or carry the groceries from the car - and I *loved* it, playing up to his attentions, keen to answer all the personal questions he asked, reveling in the way his eyes traveled over me.

"Be careful," Nicole yawned over coffee one morning. We were both tired, having stayed up way too late at a going away party MSF had thrown for her and Loic the evening before. They were leaving Kampala for Malawi the following day.

Now, we were down in the garden supervising Makena and Pierre. Both well into toddlerhood by then, they required constant supervision. This morning's antics involved trying to eat whatever flowers and leaves they managed to tear from the plants with their chubby little hands.

"Seriously," she continued, picking some petals from Pierre's lips as he squirmed in protest. "That relationship will get you in trouble."

"Oh, come on. What are you talking about?"

"You know exactly what I'm talking about."

"I haven't done anything but talk to him."

"You talked so much that you didn't even notice that Tano danced all night with other women."

"Who? Pia?"

"Yes, Pia. *And* Estelle."

Estelle, an athletic Swiss woman with a sporty, cropped haircut, was a new nurse freshly arrived from Paris. With her hysterical, shrill laugh she hardly seemed a threat.

"What difference does it make? I talked to Jacques. Tano danced with Pia and Estelle and God knows who else. Big deal. They *work* together."

Nicole raised her eyebrows.

"Besides, I'm sure Estelle is a lesbian."

"*On verra,*" she replied skeptically.

But I brushed away her insinuation. "Jacques is leaving, anyway. It's not like anything can happen." My throat tightened. "I'm more concerned about what I'm going to do without *you*."

"At least you won't be alone with Mabel."

We laughed. Tano had finally decided to let go of Mabel when he witnessed her weaving across the kitchen one day to show me the long grey string that she wore around her waist.

"This is for good luck," she'd said, her voice raspy from cigarettes.

While the string didn't faze him, the fact that she was visibly drunk and kissing all over Makena did. In the end it was a win-win situation, because she was offered a handsome severance package – a months salary for every year worked (in her case ten) - and she took the money and moved north to jumpstart her lifelong dream of opening a restaurant.

"Thank God that chapter has ended," I said, feeling the first twinges of the guilt that would later engulf me, when I finally had enough distance from the whole situation to see how Mabel, though addled and weird, was moreso than anything a symbol of my unresolved trauma.

The next morning, Nicole and I clung to each other at the airport. "I'm going to miss you more than you know," I cried.

"We'll meet again. I'm sure of it," she whispered. "Someday we'll meet. In Paris. Yes, let's meet again in Paris."

Little did we know, that fantasy was closer than either of us could have imagined.

A few days later I pulled into the driveway, radio blaring, energized from a productive day in Ssembabule. But when I turned off the engine and the music fell silent, all I could hear was Makena, howling in the back of the house.

"Tano?" I shouted, running through the door.

"Back here! Come help us!"

In the bathroom of our bedroom, Jacques held my screaming daughter in a tight grip as Tano tackled her pudgy arm.

"What on earth are you doing?"

"I'm trying to remove this tumbo larva," Tano said, "We already got two. There's just this last one…"

Since we'd moved to Kansanga, it was Makena's third bout with the flesh-eating larva. The fly laid its eggs on clothes drying in the open air. When the unsuspecting owner put on the infested article, the eggs would hatch on the skin, the larva burrowing just underneath the surface. A pimple-like bump followed that over the course of days would ripen as the larva turned into a worm.

The way to get rid of the larva once it was implanted was by suffocation, either by painting nail polish or Vaseline on the boil. It was a disgusting sight to witness, a worm gasping for breath under the surface of the skin. When the worm died, all you had to do was squeeze and *ploop!* Out slid the corpse.

"All" you had to do. Makena absolutely despised being put through the "treatment protocol" as Tano called it, and it was never anything less than a major blood curdling battle.

"Let me," I said, taking my tear stained daughter from Jacque's arms. She stopped crying immediately, and Tano quickly moved in for the kill, pressing down on the boil in one fell swoop.

While he worked, he sang a little jingle, something in Spanish that he often recited to Makena. So I barely noticed when, in the same singsong, he added, "Headquarters called this morning. About a job in Paris."

"Ummmmhumm," I said, watching as the dreaded worm emerged.

"They want me to take it."

The worm popped out and Makena resumed screaming. But by then it had registered.

"Did you say PARIS?"

He stopped singing. "Ummmmmhum."

This time it was Tano's turn to be distracted. He was busy dropping the worm into a glass of water. Once in, three of them, the size of pin heads, wiggled and squirmed in what looked like some desperate headless dance. He held the glass up to the light and squinted at it. "I'm going to keep them and see if they turn to flies."

Jacques laughed but I was impatient. "What about Paris?"

"There's nothing to tell. Headquarters said there's a place for me in the Paris office whenever I want."

My heart was pounding. Paris would be perfect. An international city. But a neutral territory. We could plant some *roots,* find some equilibrium — for Makena...for *us*...

"They probably want you to do as I do," Jacques said to Tano. "Back and forth. It has some advantages."

"Oh, please!" I said, already giddy with excitement.

But we were forced to put the conversation on hold when a rumbling noise, followed by a strong odor, emanated from Makena's diaper. As if to ensure his attention, Makena batted at Tano's face and bubbled, "Poo poo papa."

Jacques ducked out of the bathroom, and I made a move to follow him, leaving Tano with the dirty work. But as I left I said, "We don't have to decide now." I tried to sound calm. But the sight of the worms squiggling in the glass led me to plead, just a little.

"You will tell them that you are considering the offer, won't you Tano? Please keep that door open. For me. For *us*."

In the weeks that followed, Paris dangled before me like a meaty bone just out of reach of a hungry animal, in much the same way of my attraction to Jacques. Yet both Paris and Jacques, for the time at least, seemed completely unobtainable.

Once again I was completely dependent on Tano to relocate me geographically. I tried to cajole him into accepting the offer. But unlike our last two moves, this time I *really* wanted to go…and he seemed disinterested, at best.

As for Jacques, well, he had gone back to Amsterdam…although not before confirming that our attraction was mutual.

"I have a bad habit of falling for the wrong women," he'd said, early one morning, just minutes from his departure to the airport. He looked at me so intentionally that my face got hot, and I'd had to look away.

"I'll write to you from Europe," he said, before he brushed his lips against mine.

Then he was gone. As was my husband, who left minutes later for Omugo, a voyage that would last for several weeks, weeks in which we did not even speak to each other. Was this because of poor telecommunications? That was Tano's favorite excuse, even though I knew the bases in Omugo and Ibba had satellite phones which other more uxorious cowboys like Loic had used freely to keep in touch with their spouses.

Or was it because I outright discouraged the contact? Because now it was actually easier to be out of touch, as a galvanic exchange of emails broke out between Jacques and me, messages that were flirtatious, confessional, sensual....an affair based on the written word and some fantastical idea that a real relationship could someday take place. *If I weren't married. If we lived in the same place. If if if....*

After the initial flurried outpouring, however, our exchange settled into a simmering détente, when the reality that we were not likely to meet again any time soon set in. MSF needed Jacques in Kurdistan, and even my wildest imagination could not produce a credible excuse for traveling there to meet him.

I was resigned. But I was also too busy to dwell on it. In Ssembabule we were hosting a retreat every week, and I was stretched between supervising the counselors, managing the budget, and providing reports to headquarters in Minnesota and the foundation in Boston.

And another project had also taken shape. Observing the counselors and the clients in Ssembabule sitting on uncomfortable wooden benches under a tree one day, it had occurred to me: Why not turn Zoa's empty house into a counseling center?

All it would take to transform it from a modest personal residence to a warm, professional environment was a fresh coat of paint, a few new chairs and cushions, a pretty wooden sign nailed to the outside wall, and the approval, of course, of headquarters in Minnesota and village elders from around the district.

Approval secured, the MIHV team worked towards this goal over a few months, and then finally the day arrived: We were ready to officially open *The Cecie Goetz Counseling and Community Resource Center*, the new home of the Ssembabule AIDS Counseling Service.

The bedrooms where I had once spent sleepless nights were now private counseling rooms, furnished with desks and comfortable chairs. The living room had been transformed into a waiting room and resource library, with chairs and a bench, and shelves stocked with books and pamphlets in both English and Luganda on health related matters. The walls were decorated with posters about nutrition, vaccinations, and HIV prevention. Above the doorway we hung a framed photo of Cecie.

The decision to make use of Zoa's home, to honor her slain friend and to offer forth something to the local community that I was sure both women would have approved of, filled me with a sense of purposeful pride. The day of the inauguration, I wore my Directorial role with an ease I hadn't felt at Eva's funeral, and offered an emotional tribute to Cecie that acknowledged all she had done for the Ssembabule community and how loved she had been by the MIHV team. The ceremony was also an opportunity to offer elaborate praise to the SACS counselors and to recruit participants for the retreat program. Then, without further ado, we hung the wooden sign with Cecie's name on it, ceremoniously cut the ribbon stretched across the front door, and the singing and dancing began.

But before long the attention of the crowd turned to the blackening sky. The grasshoppers were arriving: hundreds of thousands of them, in a swirling mass. In a matter of hours they would touch down to earth like a tornado. While the insects were a delicacy coveted by the Ugandans, who awaited their yearly arrival in a swarm that the people rushed to collect, fry and then gobble up – or better still, *sell*, for profit -- I did not share this exotic taste, such that as soon as I could politely make a break, I jumped into the car and took off for Kampala, terrified of being on the road when the bugs rained down to the earth.

One summer evening, when the topic was no longer something I even bothered him with, Tano brought it up again: *Paris*. We had just finished a late supper on the patio, the lights of Ggaba Hills twinkling in the distance, Makena long asleep.

"I've been emailing with Frédéric Dubois," Tano said.

An intimate, homey scene flashed behind my eyes. *That lovely garret...*

"He's selling his apartment."

I sighed. "I guess we'll never get to stay there again."

"Actually," Tano said, "I thought we should consider buying it. He needs to sell fast and the market is very much in our favor right now...."

"What? I don't under—"

"I decided to accept the job." He smiled broadly.

"You're kidding." My voice sounded like it was coming from far away. *"Why?"*

"Well among other reasons, because I knew it was important to you."

I was in too much of a state of shock to reply.

"And the job suits me," he continued. "I'll be traveling a lot. But I'll continue to be in charge of the sleeping sickness trial."

"OK," I breathed, afraid that if I said more he'd change his mind.

"But if we do this," he said, "we'll have to buy a place."

Did he think that was going to upset me?

"Because I refuse to throw every paycheck away on rent. And buying, well, it's going to take every bit of our savings…and a big bank loan. But at least it will be *ours*."

I looked at him, and for a long moment we held each other's gaze. Then I flew out of my chair and into his lap. "Thank you, Tano. *Thank you thank you thank you.*"

The next morning I lounged in bed, snuggling with Makena, who had joined me with a pile of storybooks. I read to her offhandedly, but inside, I was luxuriating between thoughts of Paris and afterimages of the physical rapprochement that had taken place with Tano. An embrace on the patio had later escalated to zealous gropes, and it was over almost before it had started, both of us left breathless, relieved.

I leaned back in the pillows, wondering if it might happen again – *tonight?* - hoping it would, when Tano burst in.

"There's an Ebola outbreak in Gulu."

My skin went to goosebumps. Ebola was one of the deadliest and most contagious viruses in the world. It could be transmitted just by *touching* an infected person…and there was no known cure. I hugged Makena to me as Tano threw things into his duffel bag.

"How many people have it so far?"

"We don't have the numbers yet."

"Papa going bye bye?" Makena asked.

"Yes, darling."

"Papa never coming back?"

My eyes met Tano's. He put down his bag and sat on the edge of the bed.

"*Mi amor*," he said, cupping Makena's face in his hand. "I *will* come back."

Then, as though he could read my mind, he looked directly at me and said, "Don't worry – we'll take the most extreme precautions."

In the early days of the Ebola outbreak, several hundred people died in spite of the massive epidemic control efforts. MSF encircled the entire Gulu Hospital with plastic sheeting to control any movement in and out of the building. The guards and decontamination personnel - stationed at the only access point to the hospital - wore chlorine canisters on their backs and sprayed anyone and any object leaving the hospital. Anyone interacting with patients had to wear full protective clothing, including masks and double layers of latex gloves.

But the fatigue and stress of the epidemic caused carelessness amongst even the most educated members of the medical community, and several doctors and nurses got infected and died - including the director of the Gulu Hospital who had stayed at the front lines, caring for patients when many of his colleagues and support staff fled. His death affected the morale of the country and the international community who was trying to stop the epidemic.

A massive public education campaign was launched to help curb the epidemic. And although Ebola had not spread out of Gulu, the Ebola handshake - designed to protect people from touching each other - did. Instead of clasping hands in greeting, each person made a fist and then pushed it towards the fist of the person they were saying hello to, as though they were going to punch hands, stopping just short of actually touching.

"Greetings! Ebola handshake!" People in Kampala called out to each other, punching their fists into the air. It was a gesture people took seriously, even though no one really expected to face the virus which was thought of as "their" problem, the Northerners in Gulu.

I went to Ssembabule a few weeks into the epidemic to tell the MIHV staff and SACS counselors that I would be resigning because of our upcoming move to Paris.

"We will miss you," they said.

"I will miss you, too. I'll miss all of you. And I will come back to say goodbye with a proper hug when Ebola has passed."

But that evening Tano called home to tell me that the news had gone from bad to worse. "Ebola is now in Mbarara," he said. "I'm on my way there. Stay home with Makena while we see how this unfolds. No visitors."

"Why is this any worse than when it was in Gulu?" Mbarara was still three hours by car from Kampala.

"Because the first identified patient in Mbarara had never even traveled outside of the city."

"So?"

"So the virus had to have been carried in by someone else. But to get from Gulu to Mbarara, whoever that was, they would have had to have gone through Kampala."

"Oh shit." I suddenly understood. Kampala was the largest urban setting in Uganda. If someone contagious had come through Kampala, there was a real possibility of a countrywide pandemic.

In Mbarara, the disease investigation team quickly uncovered that Ebola had spread from the north when a soldier from Gulu who was stationed in Mbarara returned to Gulu to visit his family. He had arrived back to Mbarara – via Kampala- just as his symptoms – and therefore his infectiousness - were beginning. The high level of public awareness, rapid epidemic response measures, and some greater act of grace made it that in Mbarara only five people got infected with Ebola.

They all died.

"*Felicitations,*" the Consul General at the French Embassy said, shaking first my hand and then Tano's. It was three months later and we had just signed the papers that made the purchase of Frédéric Dubois' apartment official.

As we drove back to Kansanga, I couldn't stop saying, "I can't believe we own an apartment in Paris!"

"Well you better believe it," Tano said, "Because every last *centime* of our savings just went into it. We'll have to be even more careful with money now that we have this mortgage."

When we got home it was already early evening. Tano started towards his office but I stopped him.

"Don't *work*," I cajoled. "Let's *celebrate*. Wait there." I ran to the kitchen. I had splurged on a bottle of champagne, popping it in the freezer just before we'd left for the French Embassy.

We drank a toast on the patio.

"To new beginnings," I said. As he touched his glass to mine, I felt contrite. He had no idea how loaded that statement was.

Tano retreated to his office a few minutes later, but I stayed on the patio, refilling my glass and thinking back over these last months. After that impetuous moment of reconciliation, we had retreated again to our separate corners, maintaining an amiable but dispassionate coexistence over shared meals, parenting duties, and collegial discussions about our work.

By the time Tano emerged from his office, the champagne bottle was empty and I was lightheaded.

"I'll tuck Makena in," he said. She had fallen asleep on the sofa.

I floated to the office to check my email. There were several messages related to work that I decided to leave for the morning. But just as I was about to sign off, it popped up: a message from Jacques Rivière.

I almost didn't dare open it, painfully aware of the relative proximity of Paris to Amsterdam – four hours by train - something I had avoided thinking about, incongruent as it was with making a new start with Tano. But what was I going to do – ignore him?

I clicked on the message:

I heard that a move to Paris is underway. I dream of seeing you again. Please let me know when you will arrive.

He signed it with a thousand kisses.

Oh God, I breathed, reading the message again, the words emblazoning themselves in my head.

I heard Tano's footsteps, and I clicked off my computer, intense feelings of guilt washing over me. I felt suddenly *desperate* - for something to *happen*, some movement that would transfer all the electrifying feelings that a mere message from Jacques provoked back over to my marriage.

Then Tano was before me. "Are you alright?" he said. "You look like you're in pain."

I took his hand, ignoring his question, and led him through the house, to our bedroom. He reached for the light switch but I stopped him.

"What are you doing?"

"I wanted to tell you..." I faltered.

"What is it?"

"I wanted to tell you how much I'm looking forward to Paris."

I took his hand and put it to my heart. We stood like that for a moment, but then he broke away, saying "I have things to do," and his words provoked an unbearable fear that it was already too late - for us, for our marriage, for our family.

I began to cry, quietly at first until I could no longer contain it, loud bursting sobs breaking the silence of our room.

"Shhh!" he whispered, not unkindly, coming back towards me. "The guard will hear you!" He pulled me to his chest.

"I'm sorry," I choked.

Tano's hands were strong around my back. But he was not caressing me, he was gripping me, somehow urgently, the way someone might grip a person who was dying, right before they slipped away.

"Shhh," he whispered, "Shhhhh."

"I'm truly sorry," I repeated, pouring all the sorrow and regret of how it had turned out between us into these words, too much of a coward to state out loud the details of my remorse. He didn't answer, but for holding me tightly, until my tears slowed down and my breathing fell into an even sync with his.

The following day when Tano had left for a meeting at MSF, I sat down to write back to Jacques. I reread his message, staring at the words, deciding how to respond. It was not so long ago that I would have done just about anything to have even two minutes with him. But I knew that I couldn't carry on like this. Tano had given me Paris. I had to at least try.

I took a deep breath and typed:

Jacques
So much to tell you. Let's meet in Paris for a coffee. I should be there soon – in the next couple months. I'll let you know.

I hesitated for a moment and then added:

A thousand kisses back to you

In spite of my resolve, I didn't want to break up with him over the internet. And the thousand kisses, well, it was an exaggeration of course. But it was hard to relinquish the fantasy that had been burning inside me all these months. So I'd probably give him one or two if I could when we said our goodbyes.

I pressed SEND.

I never questioned Tano's hectic travel schedule for the sleeping sickness study. But when he suddenly undertook another clinical trial - to look at the efficacy of malaria treatments in a northern Ugandan town called Bundi Bugyo - I got annoyed.

"*Another* study? When are we *moving*? The new apartment has been empty for months."

"I can't leave Uganda until Epicentre finds my replacement."

"Are they even looking?" I argued. "And how are they going to know that you're serious about leaving if you keep taking on new projects?"

"It's my job. I don't get to just pick and choose what I do."

"Well I'm getting sick and tired of sitting around here like this."

I had stopped working weeks earlier, when someone that seemed like a good replacement came through looking for a job. MIHV did not have enough of a budget to keep us both on staff, so as Zoa had done with me more than a year earlier, I handed over the position. It had been hard to let go, but Paris was right around the corner. Or so I had thought.

"I never gave you a date. And you know how it is with my work. If you're in such a hurry why don't you go on ahead of me?"

He left again for Bundi, and for a few days I mulled over his suggestion. In my mind, we were supposed to touch down in Paris together, a family united. But if I let his work schedule set the time line for the move, Lord only knew how long I'd be waiting.

I decided to start packing.

I had just begun to assemble some cardboard boxes with a roll of heavy duty MSF logistical tape when the phone rang. It was Kavita, calling from Nairobi.

"Turn on the TV."

"What is it?"

"Some airplanes have crashed into the World Trade Center. The USA is under attack."

For a few weeks after 9/11 I staggered around in a daze. I watched the Twin Towers collapse over and over on CNN, unable to tear my eyes away from the images. I cried easily, frequently, and with no outside activity to structure my time, I found it hard to perform even the most mundane tasks, like eating, getting dressed…Even taking care of Makena was a strain, and while she was the one thing that got me up and mobilized every day, inside my spirits were dragging.

To make matters worse, since September 11th, Tano had been in Bundi Bugyo. I had called him a few times, but he continued to protest running up bills on the satellite phone, and our communication had been strained. So one day when I really felt like I was going to crack, I called Kavita in Nairobi.

"Get yourself to Paris, girl," she said. "You need to take care of *yourself*."

Thank God for girlfriends, I thought later that afternoon as I put Makena down for a nap. One word from Kavita had been enough to convince me.

The boxes I'd been taping together the day the Twin Towers were hit were stacked neatly – still empty - in the corner. I pulled one from the pile and began taking books off the shelf.

When I finished, I went into Tano's office. He had made a space for all my counseling materials, and I thumbed through them pensively. The Tropical Diseases Encyclopedia was also on the shelf – I seemed to be the only one who looked at it – and I decided to pack it as well.

As I lowered it into the box something fell from between the pages.

An envelope. I picked it up and glanced inside. Photographs. Of a clinic. Rural. Ramshackle. Patients sharing beds. There was Estelle, the Swiss nurse. Even at work she projected an image of sporty athleticism, like she was about to go jogging, rather than jab the syringe she was holding into the arm of the patient whose face had not made it into the frame of the photo.

Was she gay? I wondered, peering more closely at the photos. I really didn't know, and probably never would. I'd never see her again. Anyway, it was just a silly curiosity. I glanced mindlessly though the rest of the stack.

But the medical theme was suddenly missing from the pictures, which had evolved into several variations on her in a...*bikini?*

The reality of what I was seeing seeped through me slowly, like a shot of Novocain, such that when I got to the last photo of the pile – Tano and this *woman* shoulder to shoulder under a *matoke* tree – I was numb.

I wish I could say that I stayed frozen; that I controlled my jealousy, knowing, in fact, that it was totally unreasonable, given the way I had been carrying on with Jacques.

But what really happened is that I went crazy, screamingly, ragefully mad; an anger that exploded all boundaries.

Tano drove like a bat out of hell back to Kampala. But by the time he arrived, my one way ticket was already purchased. And without further ado, I packed up my daughter, and my bag, and I left.

PARIS

The apartment in Paris – *our* apartment – was more wonderful than I had remembered: polished oak floors, dark wooden beams in the wall between the living room and bedrooms, a huge gilded mirror above a black marble fireplace. Frédéric had left some basic furniture behind - a double mattress, a futon sofa, a bookshelf with a small black and white TV - and as I walked slowly through the apartment, barely thirty six hours after finding the photos, all I could think was *Thank God for Paris.* Overnight it had become an escape hatch.

I plunked Makena down on the bed and went to the bathroom to wash my face, a sense of satisfaction at the sound of my shoes on the wood floor. *Click. Clack.* It was a crisp, clean noise, *efficient*, not unlike the way my marriage had suddenly ended.

I pulled back my hair and stared at myself in the tiny mirror above the sink. My eyes were tired, bloodshot - I'd barely slept at all since learning of Tano's affair – and my thoughts circled around those last hours in Kampala.

Tano had pleaded as I'd packed my bag. He'd been so lonely, he said. And we'd been so estranged. And every time we'd had a little moment of rapprochement, his hopes had lifted. But we'd always gone straight back to being so distant from each other.

The shock of his words had cut through my anger.

All along he'd been feeling exactly as I had?

How was it possible that we had lived this way for years, yet never been able to talk about it?

What had happened to us?

What had we done to each other?

Makena's whimpering from the bedroom broke into my thoughts. I splashed water on my face, reaching for a towel that wasn't there. Another thing I'd need to buy. Starting from scratch. *Again.* I wiped my face on my shirt and went back to the bedroom, stretching out on the bed with my child.

We needed to sleep. *I* needed to sleep. I pulled Makena close, kneading her plump, dimply legs as she snuggled into me, her little fist clutching the chain that dangled from my neck. On it hung a pendant: a four leaf clover, pressed into a small oval of glass. Tano had handed it to me at the airport.

"I bought this for you in France months ago. I should have given it to you then. I don't know why I didn't."

A final talisman as I left African soil.

Makena purred sleepily, twisting and untwisting my chain, her eyes fixed on my face. Her downy blond hair had thickened and she had a mouthful of teeth. At two and a half, she was no longer a baby.

I must have dozed off, because suddenly I was in a dream, swimming the length of an Olympic size pool. I was the only one in the water and I was moving fast, strong, powerful strokes slicing me forward until I reached the deep end. As I hoisted myself from the water, I woke up, feeling oddly energized.

Where was the sorrow? I pulled Makena closer still. By now she was in a deep slumber, my baby girl who was growing up. I was growing up, too. Or maybe it was an act already completed? Because in that moment, in spite of all the reasons I had to be worried, all I really felt was triumphant.

We were in Paris!

Soon we had our daily routine worked out. It was really quite simple: I fastened Makena into her new *poussette*, and we wandered, without a plan, from our front door on rue Oberkampf, where, as if in a fairytale, we tread across a carpet of petals that the flower shop next door sprinkled on the sidewalk every morning.

I inhaled the city in great, greedy gulps, filling my lungs with its sublime landscape, its winding streets and elegant architecture that imposed a sense of majesty. Paris filled me with promise: I detected it in the meticulous window displays, the artisanal chocolate shops, the bistros whose tables spilled out onto the sidewalk, their stylish, chain-smoking patrons huddling for warmth under heat lamps.

Ten minutes down the street, right off *Place de la Bastille* was an internet dive called Café Liberté, run by an expressionless Korean man, who, in spite of our twice daily forays to his establishment, never once said hello with any indication that he recognized us. But I didn't mind. It was the antithesis of being the spotlighted *muzungu*, and I reveled in his indifference, grateful for the chance to get on with my business and not have to be at the center stage of curiosity or covetousness.

My "business" was sending emails to every contact I had – close or remote - around France, and at any French institutions in the United States to ask: Does anyone have suggestions for where a clinical social worker from the United States of America might find work in Paris?

Working papers in order, I always clarified in bold, knowing that without mention of the requisite *permis de travail* I probably wouldn't even get an answer. There were an estimated 80,000 Americans living in Paris, not to mention all the other thousands of English speaking hopefuls who came to Paris in search of *la vie en rose*. But "making it" in France without papers was virtually impossible, unless one was ready to function on the black market. So while I didn't have my papers *yet*, I would, as soon as Tano's were processed, which required his presence on French soil...which required Epicentre finding his replacement and/or a sign from me that I was ready to see him.

Which came first remained to be seen.

But regardless of my legal *right* to work, the answers to my queries were pessimistic:

Never mind if you have papers - the French economy is so bad you'll never find a job anyway.

If you don't have a French degree, it's impossible to get work.

Social work in France is not the same as social work in the United States.

You'll never make it. Come back to America where life is easy.

I understood: loved ones in the States just wanted us back. Only the friends I'd made as an MSF wife - Kavita and Nicole – were optimistic about my idea to stay in Paris.

And, of course, Tano, who bombarded me with phone calls and emails that overflowed with apologies and plans that broke completely from the "team" mentality that had always defined him. Now he made promises of intimate, homely time, *en couple* and *en famille*. He wanted to talk about *furniture*, and did I have enough money to choose a sofa from the IKEA catalogue as I had so often talked about?

As for the discouraging messages from the French themselves, I refused to take them seriously. They were notorious for their complaining, negative attitude. I knew that already from my interactions with Guillaume. But even in the month I'd been here, the number of *manifs* – protests – was astonishing. The French had no idea how good they had it: free health care, a system of *allocations familiales*, a government benefit to offset the costs of raising children, subsidized child care (Makena had already been offered twenty hours per week in the cheerful crèche up the road)...All of these possibilities were open to us as soon as our residency papers were processed.

And in France, regardless of legal status, one could even get free therapy.

The *Centre Medico-Psychologique*, or *CMP*, was a government sponsored psychiatric and therapy service that had branches in every *arrondissement* in Paris. Shortly after our arrival, I made an appointment with one Dr. Benlolo at the *CMP* in our *quartier*, just off of Avenue de la République.

I went to the first meeting with visions of pleasant therapy offices past in my mind. Like most medical establishments in Paris, the address was in an old Hausmannian building, with an elegant iron grille and a code at the door. Just beyond the refined exterior, however, I was taken aback by the urine saturated foyer and the sight of two drunken men clutching each other and weaving down the stairs. I stepped aside, hugging Makena to me.

From the looks of the other people in the waiting room, the *CMP* was clearly utilized by the indigent of Paris: bums played cards or snoozed in the old plastic chairs. I could tell the receptionist was surprised by my comparatively well-to-do appearance. When she heard my accent she said, in French, "Dr. Benlolo does not speak English."

But this was not a problem for me anymore, as the years in Anglophone East Africa had catapulted me to near fluency in French, an unforeseen benefit of the constant presence of the francophone MSF team.

I sat down to wait, Makena on my lap. A tiny woman with deep set eyes and an angular face stared at us, periodically twitching and jerking and muttering "merde!" *Tourettes?* It wasn't funny, I knew, but when she suddenly released a long, loud belch, I couldn't stifle my laughter.

At that moment a small man with olive skin and silver-rimmed spectacles appeared.

"Madame Duncombe?" He offered his hand. *Dr. Benlolo.*

I followed him down the shabby corridor to his office. He gestured for me to sit down and as he took his place behind a large wooden desk, my eyes swept over the room. It was sparsely furnished: a medical examination table, a scale, a small box of toys, two wooden chairs. I set Makena down in front of the toys and took a seat.

"How can I help you, Madame?" he asked, leaning forward on his desk, his hands folded meticulously in front of him. A blank file folder just like the ones I had imposed on the Teenage Clinic at Kenyatta Hospital lay on his desk. I closed my eyes and imagined a long list of notes about me that might end up written there: 32 years old, mother of one, history of trauma, depression, anxiety, former trailing wife...

"Madame?"

I opened my eyes. "It's a long story."

"Why don't you start at the beginning?"

Down the hallway I heard someone ranting; the tiny woman belched again. But this time I didn't laugh. Instead, I took off as though I were running, wanting to tell him everything: about moving to Africa when I was ten, about changing countries every few years and feeling totally rootless, about how I'd relinquished all my plans when I met Tano because doing what he wanted felt more normal to me than chasing my own dreams. How I'd really tried to pull a life together in East Africa...but the anxiety post-carjacking had made everything so difficult. How I wanted to start over, in Paris. But there was Tano's affair. And there was mine. We had fucked everything up.

Dr. Benlolo didn't say a word while I spoke. He barely moved at all, except to pass me the tissues when I cried. When I finished talking he picked up a pen and wrote my name on the folder. Then he jotted some notes on a piece of paper and slid it inside.

"Sounds like you had your own personal September 11th," he said. Then he shook my hand. "Come in next Thursday. We can start sorting it all out."

A few days later, I sat before the computer at Café Liberté, bracing myself for more messages about why I should not stay in France one second longer.

But when my inbox booted up on the screen, it indicated that since I'd checked the evening before... *thirty six emails had come in?*

It had to be junk mail, I reasoned, scanning down the list, expecting to see promises of miracle cures for weight loss and libidinal boosters. Yet the subject headings were all personal, as though they could have even pertained to me.

> *Fabulous news about the divorce*
> *Sent the money — Did you get it?*
> *Drinks on Saturday at the Buddha Bar*
> *Weekend in Saint Tropez with Gerard*

I clicked on the first one.

Dear Shirley,

Hope life post break-up is treating you well. Stella told me about the settlement. You go, girl!

And the next:

Shirl,

We get to Paris next week. We'd like to fit in at least a couple Michelin three stars. Could you take charge of reservations?

I began rapidly opening the emails. They were *all* to Shirley, who was apparently a recent – and rich - divorcee from Dallas, Texas.

A crossed email connection? Some uncanny sense of kismet tingled inside me. Scanning through the text, I found a Paris phone number. I scribbled in my notebook, gathered up Makena, and left the Liberté.

I didn't have any credit on my phone, and impatient as I was to get to the bottom of this, I called Shirley's number from a payphone on the street. It rang seven times and then switched over to a recording. A female voice with a deep Texan drawl said *Bonjour ya'll! Leave a message!*

I offered a brief explanation of how I had gotten her number, and left her mine. But as I was saying goodbye, someone snatched up the receiver.

"Don't hang up!"

"Shirley?"

"I'll be a dog's flea," Shirley said. "Seems to me that the universe must be trying to introduce us."

I laughed. "Do you think?"

"I was just about to open a bottle of champagne. Care to join me?"

Champagne? At 11 AM?

In the far corner of the phone booth a small grey spider, like the ones I'd seen all over our house in Kampala, spun a web. It seemed so unlikely to see her there, the middle of winter in Paris, France.

"I'd love to," I answered. "Where are you?"

She started to give me directions, but when she said she was across the street from Café Liberté, I cut her off.

"I'm in a phone booth right outside."

"Well hurry on over then," she drawled.

We hung up the phone but I stayed in the booth for a moment longer watching the spider. Spinning. Surviving.

Take care, I whispered, before ducking back out into the cold.

Shirley's apartment could well have been a spread from House Beautiful, and Shirley, who could have won a Dolly Parton look-alike contest with her big bosom and frosted blonde hair, was the perfect proprietor in her silky emerald colored lounge set and high heeled mules.

"You got yourself a darlin' little girl," she fawned over Makena. "I got several myself, but they're all grown up now. Their daddy is French. He left me for a pretty young thing two years ago." She gestured to the apartment around us. "I got all this in the settlement."

"Your place is beautiful." I took a few steps into the living room. It had two plush velvet sofas arranged just so, an elegant glass coffee table between them. Heavy satin drapes framed the windows, through which there was a perfect view of the Place de la Bastille.

"Thank you. Full credit goes to my decorator. She's done all of my places."

"Oh?"

"I run a rental business." She gestured for me to sit down. "Now let's pop that bottle." She looked at her watch. "I always say if I haven't had any champagne by lunch I ain't livin' right." She poured us each a glass.

An hour later – the bottle empty – I had disclosed an abbreviated version of my life. And I'd learned some important details of hers: She owned *five* apartments around Paris that she rented out on a short term basis. The one where we currently sat was the biggest unit. It had five bedrooms and two bathrooms.

"The other four are smaller – two two-bedrooms and two studios. The smaller ones are easier to rent."

"Interesting." I tipped my glass back to get the last drop of champagne.

"Dodging bullets in Africa is what's interesting," she laughed. "What we're talking about here is luxury, honey. Just the way I like it. Now listen to me…You looking for work? Because I may have the perfect job for you."

"But I told you, I won't have my work papers in order until my husband…"

She waved my words away. "Forget him. No working papers needed for this job. I had a girl working for me, managing cleaning and maintenance staff and taking care of the guests, but she eloped down to the South of France. Just last week…The minute you walked through that door," she said, gesturing to the foyer, "I thought you'd be *perfect* for the job…"

"Me?"

"Yes. I need someone all smiley and bi-lingual." She pronounced it *baah-lingwuuul*. "Let me tell you how it works."

Becoming Shirley's apartment rental manager was a stroke of good luck that catapulted me overnight into the world of the Paris black market. She paid me in cash - one hundred euros per rental - a flat fee that included greeting the guests, showing them around the apartment and locking up behind them after they'd vacated. Any additional time spent I billed her fifteen euros per hour.

"It sounds so straightforward," I said, the day she took me on a tour of all the apartments. "I can't imagine what I'd need to bill you extra for."

"There's nothing straightforward about this business, honey. If it ain't the plumbing in these old buildings, it's the electricity. And if it ain't the electricity, it's the guests. Think *high maintenance*."

She wasn't exaggerating, I soon learned. The apartments were old and full of problems: decrepit plumbing systems, bedraggled electrical circuits....

Guests called at all hours. *The toilet exploded! You've gotta come!* Or *The lights keep turning themselves on and off!*

If I wasn't able to solve the problem myself, I turned to Shirley's "people:" two persnickety handymen, Marcel and Yannick, who smelled of wine and cigarettes no matter the time of day, and whose services required long, complicated negotiations. In spite of the headlines about the failing French economy, they seemed to resent any request for their services, puffing their cheeks out and bobbing their heads – *degouté* in spite of their handsome cash payments - about having to respond to another one of Shirley's problems.

Barely a month into the job, Yasmina, Shirley's cleaning lady, quit to attend to a family emergency back in Algeria.

"Call Marcel or Yannick," Shirley said as we shared her customary late morning bottle of champagne. "See if they got themselves any girlfriends who can take over."

But I happened to know that Yasmina earned ten euros per hour, and as the stack of earnings under my mattress grew thicker, the more stable my life as an independent woman was becoming.

"Why don't *I* handle the cleaning, Shirley?"

"A skinny little gal like you?"

"Try me," I said, the bubbles tickling my throat as they went down.

Taking on the housekeeping proved to have two benefits. One was the money, the other the therapy of physical labor, a type of meditation in which I began to seriously contemplate my professional future in Paris.

As the weeks passed and the pressure to return to "my" country with Makena mounted, my desire to stay in Paris turned into *conviction*: Leaving would be *contre coeur*. In spite of the turmoil in my personal life, I *adored* being here, armed with a new certainty that *here* I fit in, not French but not quite American either; a chronic expat who was trading in that title for *immigrant*, posing my bags and settling down for the long haul.

So as I mopped floors and wiped down counters, I mulled over *what* to do next. Although working for Shirley was a wonderfully serendipitous jump start, I knew it was only a temporary security. The dots of the last five years were now connecting, and that once baffling term – *consultant* – kept popping into my mind, smattered with images from the best parts of my professional history: the health education classes at juvenile detention in Seattle, the substance abuse clinic in New Orleans, the Teenage Clinic in Nairobi, the HIV counseling program in Ssembabule...

Paris was full of international schools like the ones I had attended, full of foreign Embassies and international clubs for expatriates...

I *knew* this community, knew it like the back of my hand, and as I ironed sheets and fluffed pillows and greeted guests like a cheerful Girl Friday, a vision of business cards, printed with my name and the title *CLINICAL SOCIAL WORKER* danced behind my smile, as did the lovely image of a sunny office, two comfortable chairs, a box of tissues...

Avoiding any promises about our potential reconciliation, I finally hinted to Tano that I was ready for him to get to France so that we could at least get our work permits in order.

"You just want me for my European passport," he joked. But the sadness in his tone betrayed the subtext of his statement: *was our marriage really over?*

I recounted the conversation to Dr. Benlolo, who I had been seeing on a twice weekly basis. I'd seen therapists before – counselors at both Mount Holyoke and Tulane, as well as when I'd first gotten out of college. But the work with Dr. Benlolo was by far more productive than any of my past therapies. There was something about him – some *je ne sais quoi* – that invited intimacy and insight.

"So is it over?" he asked. "Can you *really* imagine a life without Tano?"

The way he peered at me, over the rim of his glasses, as though he knew the answer already and just wanted to see if I could guess correctly, sent a ripple of angst from my stomach up through my throat.

The truth was that deep down, I *missed* Tano, missed his intensity, his intellectual fire, his quiet assuredness. I missed having him there as a back up for Makena, who babbled frequently about Papa, and who emulated him in play – "drinking *mate*" from a plastic toy, playing guitar with an old badminton racket we'd found on the sidewalk in front of our apartment.

But I was so *furious* - at him, at myself, and at this system we had entered into that had subsumed my life to his. It was all so insidious, such that now, when I found myself fantasizing kissing and making up, those romantic musings turned quickly to paranoia. If I took him back, what would happen to me? Before I knew it would I be on another non-stop flight to some tropical danger zone?

When I didn't answer, Dr. Benlolo said, "And Jacques?"

"What about him?" I yanked a tissue from the box and began shredding it.

"You tell me."

"I don't have anything to tell," I snapped, childishly, revealing the tension I felt every time I thought about my own unconsummated affair. I knew I needed to tell Tano, but when was the right moment? Would it come across as mere vindictiveness if I announced it so soon after discovering his infidelity?

"I wonder what things would be like now if Tano had agreed to leave Nairobi when you asked him to."

"Meaning?"

Dr. Benlolo shrugged. "Just wondering."

"We would have gone to the next mission, I guess."

"*Oui?*"

Suddenly my head was filled with an image of a former me - standing before Tano and begging *him* to make a change so that something in *my* life could change. Just remembering how dependent I'd felt made me shudder.

"I suppose that if he had agreed to leave Nairobi, I probably wouldn't be in Paris right now." I mashed the filmy strips of tissue into a ball. Then I looked Dr. Benlolo in the eyes. "If Tano had made things easier for me, I might never have learned to stand on my own two feet."

3:30 AM. The ringing of the phone woke me from a deep sleep. *Please don't be an exploding toilet* I prayed, fumbling for the receiver. "Hello?" My voice came out in a croak.

No answer.

"*Hello?*"

"Is that you, girl?"

"Kavita?" I sat up in bed. "Where are you?"

"In Nairobi. I'm sorry for calling so late, but I leave for India tomorrow and wanted your news."

We hadn't spoken since I'd started working for Shirley, so I told her all about my foray in the Paris tourist rental world.

"And now you're finally going to get your practice started, too," Kavita said.

"*Thinking* of getting it started."

"Forgive me, girl, but you *are* getting it started: With the International Women's Club. Next month."

It took me a second to understand: She wasn't asking. She was telling.

"The IWC in Paris needs a speaker."

"And?"

"I signed you up."

"What?"

"Long story short, I traded business cards with a woman named Jacqueline on a flight from London to Mombasa last week. Very nice woman. Powerful husband. Corporate."

"Cut to the chase."

"On the flight she told me all about the IWC and said that one of their main functions is to help executive's wives get settled in France."

"What does this have to do with me?"

"I said you'd be a great resource."

"I'm going to kill you."

"Why? You know firsthand what being a trailing wife is like."

"Just because I was one doesn't mean that I'm equipped—"

"And I told her you're a therapist."

"Kavita, I'm scrubbing toilets for a living."

"You're doing what you need to for the time being. You *are* a therapist. That doesn't go away just because you have a client base or you don't. Do you think Tano stops being a doctor from one day to the next? That's your *identity*, girl. Be who you are."

I eyed the clock. 4:15. And I had to let some people in to one of Shirley's units at 8. Next to me Makena began to stir. "OK, talk quick."

"Apparently they have a spring conference and their keynote speaker's husband has just been transferred to China, so she's no longer available. They need someone to talk about trailing. I gave her your mobile number. You'll undoubtedly hear from her soon."

Jacqueline called the very next day, just as I was leaving the new renters *ooohing* and *aaahing* over Shirley's stylish apartment. It was a family of three who had arrived with luggage for thirty – *heavy luggage* – which I had single-handedly lugged up the stairs.

I stood in the stairwell, rubbing my shoulder, Makena yanking at my sweater and fussing, as Jacqueline spoke. I pressed the phone tightly to my ear.

"You come *highly* recommended by your associate, Ms. Kavita Quereshi."

My associate? I had to remember to repeat that one back to Kavita.

"We have a membership of 250 women from 30 different countries. Ms. Quereshi explained that you specialize in working with international expatriate families."

I cleared my throat. "Yes, in fact, I'm particularly interested in working with *accompanying* spouses. I specialize in depression, anxiety, adjustment difficulties, identity questions…"

I stopped, amazed by how fluently this statement just tumbled out of my mouth. Even Makena stopped whining, looking at me with round eyes.

"Well these are absolutely the areas of interest to our group," Jacqueline said. She sounded impressed. "May I ask how you ended up in Paris?"

I wondered if she could hear the smile in my voice as I gave a sterilized explanation of how I went from being a Foreign Service child, to an MSF wife, to an independent professional woman in Paris. Without the gory details it actually sounded quite romantic.

"That is certainly fascinating. And what an admirable organization MSF is."

I smiled again. People would always be wowed by MSF. "Yes, they do very important work."

"And your husband sounds like a saint."

"That might be stretching it a little..."

As we laughed together I saw my life as something *live,* charged with possibility, some magical inverse of the dreaded sense of uselessness that had accompanied me, just five years earlier, to Kenya.

"Our spring conference is coming up. And we're looking for someone that could talk, from her own experience, about creating a life in a foreign country. Would you happen to have any space open in your schedule? We'd love to have you as a speaker."

As she spoke it occurred to me: *It* was gone, the old pulley system, jerking me up and down. *Envy, jealousy, resentment* – all of those painful feelings which had played such a role in my life with Tano were no longer present.

"Coping with being an accompanying spouse," she said. "What to *expect.* Pursuing personal goals..."

Jacqueline's voice brought me back from my thoughts.

"I'm sorry," I said, "What did you say?"

"The pursuit of *goals,*" she repeated. "Of course, I defer to you. You're the expert."

We hung up and I crossed the street to Café Liberté. I wanted to send Kavita – *my associate, Ms. Quereshi* - an email of thanks.

I had a gig!

And a string of ideas were already zipping in and out of my head: how to structure the presentation, the lessons I had learned...

My thoughts drifted to East Africa, all that I had been unprepared for and all that I had worked through. It would certainly blow poor Jacqueline's mind if I stood before the lunching ladies of the IWC and explained that I'd "coped" with being an accompanying spouse by smoking pot, popping prozac, having an affair...

I closed my eyes, remembering. I hadn't contacted Jacques since leaving Uganda, hadn't been ready, aware, once I was away from Tano that it would likely look like I was on the rebound, looking to start over as soon as possible.

And of course that had occurred to me. But whatever I had tried to imagine as a potential scenario – me with my new French husband, living in Amsterdam – I couldn't quite get it out of the bedroom and into real life. What would it be like to clip my toenails with Jacques standing by? What about peeing in front of him, or worse? And what about Makena? An affair was one thing, a real relationship another. And I was a package deal.

Now I stared at the keyboard, my fingers poised. Did he even have any idea that Tano and I had split up?

Glancing around the café, as though the other patrons might perceive the furtive message being concocted at my terminal, I began to type.

A few weeks later, I pushed Makena's poussette through the crowds of Gare du Nord, toward *Voie A*, where the fast train from Amsterdam had arrived at 6:30. I was ten minutes late, and rushing through the station I might have believed I was back in Kenya or Uganda, the corridors teeming with Africans, some as overloaded with packages and luggage as had been the norm on those ill-fated matatus. But these Africans spoke French – immigrants of France's former colonies: Senegal, Togo, Burkina Faso, Cote d'Ivoire - an accented patois that reminded me of my childhood in West Africa.

At the head of the *Voie* I stopped, skimming the thinned-out crowd. *Where was he?*

The elastic band I used to pull my hair back had cut a deep purple line into my wrist, and I rubbed the aggrieved flesh, feeling increasingly skittish.

Then through the crowd I saw him. We approached each other tentatively.

"I'm sorry I'm late," I said, pulling my hair back. We looked at each other, long and hard. I was more nervous than I'd realized.

"I was afraid you'd changed your mind," Jacques said, leaning in to give me *la bise*. Then he squatted down in front of Makena. She stared at him as he planted a kiss right in the center of one of her little hands.

He glanced up at me. "She really looks like Tano."

As if on some symbiotic cue at the sound of her father's name, Makena started whimpering.

Please don't, I implored silently, but rapidly her cries escalated to furious screams.

I suddenly felt like bawling, too. *What on earth had I been thinking, inviting him here?*

Jacques led me and my howling charge through the station to the taxis, where miraculously one was available. We piled in and proceeded to the apartment at high speed, Makena screaming all the way. Jacques paid the driver and then shouted, over Makena's unrelenting cries:

"Shall I get us some dinner?"

From the glances of passersby, I imagined we looked like just another young family, embroiled in our child's tantrum. *If they only knew*, I thought, suddenly exhausted. As I dragged Makena up the stairs – the minute Jacques walked away she had fallen silent – I had an overwhelming urge to call off the whole evening.

Almost two hours later, Makena sound asleep, Jacques tapped quietly on the door. I opened it expecting to see him with a few simple cartons of take out, but he was loaded down with seven full grocery bags.

"What's all this?" I led him to the kitchen, where he emptied the contents of his arms on the counter.

"Dinner," he said, tugging me towards him in embrace. I let my head rest against the soft cotton of his shirt, breathing into his chest as he tightened his hold on me. But then I pulled back, suddenly shy, expressing my hesitation by retreating to the doorway of the kitchen.

"I'll cook," he said, unfazed. He poured me a glass of wine. Then he laid three small white onions out on the counter and one by one removed their skin.

"How are you doing?" he said as he worked.

"Fine," I answered. But as the words left my mouth, the sharp juice of the onions filled the air, brimming my eyes with tears.

"I'm not crying," I sniffled, swiping a tissue across my cheeks. "I really am *fine*." I laughed as more tears spilled down my face, remembering that old Aerosmith song that the kids in juvenile detention used to quote: *FINE, as in fucked-up, insecure, neurotic and emotional.*

That was me, alright. The epitome of fine.

"I mean, all things considered. It's not always easy being alone with Makena."

He nodded and kept chopping. In spite of my reservations, as before, something about his easy company made me want to blabber – almost like a protracted session with Dr. Benlolo. But with Jacques it was reciprocal.

"I have something to tell you," he said, lighting the fire on the stove. "Um, it's a bit awkward, but....I have a new girlfriend."

It slipped out before I could stop it: "Is she married, too?"

He laughed. "Ouch!"

"I didn't mean it that way," I said, my face turning red. "And besides, I'm in no position to judge."

"She's not married."

"So why did you come here?"

"I wanted to see you. I knew you and Tano had broken up, and I thought about calling, but I told myself that I wouldn't go behind Athena's back...."

Athena?

"Unless I heard from you, that is."

So he was involved – with the Goddess of Wisdom, no less. I was still reflecting on this when he stepped toward me. Knowing instinctively that this was the grand finale of my extramarital love life, I threw myself at him, as a death row prisoner might approach her last meal, opening my mouth to his, begging his hands to cover every last inch of my flesh.

Afterwards, we lay together on the sofa.

"So why did you ask me to come?"

I thought about it for a minute, running my fingers up and down his chest. "Loose ends, I guess. Curiosity. Opportunity. I don't know. Maybe I wanted to balance things out a little with Tano."

"So you're just using me to get revenge," Jacques joked.

I looked at him, trying to decide my answer. In some way, he was absolutely right. On the other hand, it was so much more complicated than that.

Jacques might have transformed those stinging onions into a lovely omelette, or a savory soup to be sopped up with the crusty bread that was amongst the groceries he'd purchased. But our frenzy of lovemaking and the languid conversation that followed banished any further notions of food from our thoughts, and we spent the rest of the night alternating between this intensive carnal exchange and the intimate conversation that piggybacked in on its heels.

When sunrise was near, I climbed into bed with Makena, where I plunged quickly into a dreamless sleep. A few hours later I awoke, startled by a peculiar noise, like a growling animal, coming from the other room. I sat up in bed.

Snoring.

Dear God.

It *had* been a lovely evening...but how I wished Jacques hadn't spent the night.

Next to me Makena stirred, and my thoughts flipped back to her screaming fit at the station. At least one thing was patently clear: There was no substitute for Tano when it came to dealing with Makena. Now all I wanted was for Jacques to be out of here before she woke up.

Another respiratory honk blasted from Jacque's direction. *Ugh.* Tano was a more delicate sleeper, too.

I tiptoed from the bedroom to the kitchen, where I scooped enough coffee into the filter to make ten strong cups. Then I watched as it began to drip – the periodic *hissssss* of the machine the only other sound as the last grey streaks of early morning turned blue through the window.

"Smells good," Jacques said a few moments later, resting his head on top of mine. It was affectionate, and as he lingered there, I wondered how I could gently shoo him out. But then he said, "If you don't mind, I'll catch the early train back to Amsterdam."

As soon as Jacques left, I took a hot shower, scrubbing away any lingering evidence of my infraction with the same vigor in which I stuffed its afterimages into the deep recesses of my mind. I'd deal with what it all *meant* later. For now, there was something more pressing occupying my thoughts.

With Dr. Benlolo's encouragement, I'd ordered business cards and letterhead, treating my home as my temporary business address. I had written letters to numerous international schools and embassies, offering my services as a consultant who could provide health education and counseling to teenagers and adults.

Now I folded each letter carefully, tucking them into envelopes embossed with my name. The last letter in the pile was to Phillip Davis, an American clinical social worker with more than thirty years of experience in France, who had agreed to take me on as a supervisee if and when my private practice got off the ground.

Hope to see you soon! I'd scrawled across the page.

With that last envelope licked and sealed, I turned to the most important task still at hand: My presentation for the IWC.

While I waited for my laptop to boot up, I opened my notebook. I had been scribbling out thoughts about trailing ever since the conversation with Jacqueline. Now I thumbed through the pages, covered in blue, black and red ink.

Like bruises and blood after the battle, I thought.

Then I stuck my pencil behind my ear and typed:

INTERNAL ISSUES THAT CAN BE TRIGGERED BY TRAILING

Uncertainty of purpose

Depression/anxiety/low self esteem

Identity confusion or loss

Questions about meaning of life

Well that about summed up my first month in Nairobi, didn't it? Could I assume these issues were universal?

I typed the next slide rapidly, imagining myself saying, *These issues can lead to:*

EXISTENTIAL CRISIS

What is *my* purpose?

Where do I fit in here?

Where do I fit in back home?

Who am I as a professional?

Who am I as a spouse?

Who am I as a parent?

Who am I as a person?

Being confronted with these questions can lead to

I had just started to type **Marital Difficulties** when Makena woke up. I gave her breakfast and we read some stories and then I pulled out some toys, hoping she'd play independently. But she clamored into my lap, dribbling juice and cookie crumbs all over the notes I'd spent weeks painstakingly jotting.

"Mommy is working," I explained, using my firmest tone. But to Makena, "Mommy working" meant "let's crack open the play-doh." I resorted to bribing her with the rest of the cookies, but once she'd gobbled them down she was back at me. Resigned, I turned off the computer and headed out the door, into a fine drizzle.

We had only been walking for ten minutes when it turned into a hard rain. We ducked into the nearest café, a trendy, dim environment, with swirling blue lights providing a galaxy of abstract stars on the wall. A funky, mystical soundtrack played, and Makena was mesmerized by the effect. I got us settled in a corner table and had just ordered an espresso and a *crepe au nutella* when my phone rang.

"*Querida?*"

"Tano." He had been in South Sudan and we hadn't spoken for almost three weeks.

"Epicentre found my replacement."

I pressed the phone tightly to my ear.

"I'm coming to Paris."

Was it the swirling lights of the café or actually a jolt of adrenaline that made me feel dizzy?

He must have taken my silence for dismay, because his voice cracked when he asked, "Don't you even want to see me a little bit?"

I pictured him on the other end of the line, rubbing his chin, shoulders slumped in his MSF t-shirt.

"I do, Tano. I do." I was struck by my own words: the same ones I'd uttered before the judge in New Orleans five long years ago.

If I had dared put my foot down then, would I have lost him?

But this wasn't the moment to examine old wounds. Nor was it, I thought, as the reminder of sex burned in all the muscles of my body, the moment for confession. That would come later.

For now I decided to tell him just two things, both essential for the regeneration of our marriage.

"Paris is a totally different life, Tano. And Makena and I are waiting here for you."

The night Tano arrived in Paris, I let Makena answer the door. I'll never forget how they paused upon first sight of each other. Not yet three, perhaps she had to let memory catch up with instinct; and he, the spurned family man, was likely afraid that she wouldn't remember him.

But it was only a split second, and then she cried, "Papa!" and he dropped to his knees, just in time to catch her as she leapt into his arms, holding on with what I am sure, with a mother's knowledge of her child, was dear life.

"*Mi amor,*" was all he could manage, as they rocked back and forth for the longest time.

I looked on, catapulted back for whatever mysterious reason, to one of the first dates I ever had with Tano, a few days after meeting him in New Orleans. He proposed we take a long bike ride around the perimeter of the city, from uptown to downtown and back again. I hadn't really wanted to go – I'd always been maladroit and had not been on a bike for years.

But he had "surprised" me by borrowing two bikes from his neighbors, and seemed so eager I couldn't bear to let him down. So I rode tentatively behind him, grateful that he was in the lead - less because of his superior navigation skills than for the relief that he wouldn't be able to see me tottering along. But when my wheels got caught in the tracks of the Saint Charles Street Car, I couldn't suppress a yelp as my bike stopped abruptly and I flew over the handlebars.

It couldn't have taken him more than two seconds to reach me, sprawled out and humiliated on the pavement of Saint Charles Avenue.

"*Mi amor,*" he'd said, cradling me in his arms, just like he would six years later to our own little girl.

"*Mi amor.*"

Six weeks later, I stood at the front of the conference hall at a grand hotel at *La Defense*, a modern corporate complex just outside of Paris. Approximately 75 women – all of them elegantly coiffed and dressed - sat in groups of ten, at round tables. Waiters circulated, refilling glasses with water, champagne.

The calm that I had felt reviewing my notes on the metro now evaded me: my simple linen outfit and loose chignon felt juvenile compared to all this meticulous grooming. Part of me wanted to bolt out of the hotel and take the metro straight back to the 11th arrondissement.

But a hush came over the room as the lights dimmed, except for the spotlight shining down on me, and I suddenly heard Kavita's voice: *That's your identity, girl. Be who you are.*

I began to speak. "When the man who is now my husband asked me to accompany him to East Africa, I barely even thought about what it might mean to *my* life. You know, things like career, family, *home*? I thought that love would take care of every need."

A collective titter sounded through the room.

"Sound familiar? Anyone who has moved to a foreign country to follow a spouse on *their* career path knows just how much tension can be triggered, how much this can spawn certain internal issues."

I paused, my eyes traveling over the faces of the women before me.

"You're probably used to people saying 'You're soooooo lucky' that you get to live in Paris."

Throughout the audience heads nodded *yes*.

"After all, Paris *is* the 'city of light.' But coming here on vacation is *not* the same as coming here as an accompanying spouse. So in response to other people's envy, you may find yourself thinking...."

I pulled up the first slide.

If I get to live in Paris, why am I so depressed?

More laughter.

Encouraged by the attentive expressions and the frequent nods of recognition, I moved through the presentation. Thirty minutes later, the audience of women rose to their feet in applause. Jacqueline came up on stage to shake my hand.

"*Most* useful," she murmured. "Do I have permission to give your contact information to women who might like to follow up?"

I practically floated home, caught up in the thrill of the presentation and the possibilities that Jacqueline hinted might follow. Until now, I had been enjoying the bareness of the apartment - it had seemed a natural transition from the hand me down nature of the MSF housing, and a metaphor for the skeletal remains of our relationship.

But I needed to get an office organized now, and fast.

A week later, a delivery truck pulled up and two surly drivers unloaded a girlish canopy bed and matching dresser for Makena, a plush orange and yellow rug in the shape of a sun, and a bright blue toy box. My original intention to buy furnishings for an office had been diverted when, browsing the aisles of IKEA, Shirley had called.

"Stop right there!" she said when I told her what I was doing. "I have a garage full of antiques that Stella picked up at the *puce*."

The *puce* was the *marché aux puces,* the flea market, where Shirley's decorator Stella bought all of the gorgeous antique bargains that filled Shirley's units. "Bargains" for those with money. I had analyzed my savings and had just enough extra to buy three or four simple IKEA pieces, the basic shell of a very modest office. Even one antique of the quality that Shirley and Stella dealt with would put me way over my budget for the month.

"You take what you want for your new office-"

"Oh Shirley, I couldn't afford-"

"Hear me out. You take what you want, and we'll do it like a barter. You'll be makin' your own money soon enough workin' as a psychiatrist…"

I didn't bother correcting her. No matter how many times I'd explained that a social worker was not a psychiatrist, she continued to refer to me that way, even told incoming renters that "her" psychiatrist would be meeting them at the apartment upon their arrival.

"…and I'll stop paying you the flat fee until you've paid off the furniture. Any clean up or time you spend between letting guests in and out, I'll keep you on payroll for. Sound like a deal?"

Gratitude welled inside me. *How did I get this lucky?*

I asked myself that question again, a few hours after Marcel and Yannick finished assembling Makena's new furniture. They came over as a surprise, courtesy of Shirley.

"I know you're an independent gal," she said when I called to thank her. "But let them help you. Consider it a housewarming gift from me."

Now, my daughter sleeping peacefully in her new bed, I sipped a cup of tea and leaned back in the firm padding of the armchairs I'd chosen from Shirley's garage. The patined oak of the chairs, upholstered in a rich burgundy velvet, with scrolling armrests sat beautifully on the wooden floor of my apartment. *I'd be bartering these chairs off for years*, I thought, tracing my finger along the faun's head carving that ran along the top edge of each chair.

But God, it was worth it. The "office" was gorgeous, a low oak table in between the chairs – *you can have that*, Shirley had said, *its only 100 years old* – and a simple cast iron lamp in the corner, its deep red lampshade a subtle match for the chairs.

Just in time for tomorrow. I breathed a sigh of relief. The very evening after the conference, a woman had called me. "Do you see teenagers?" she asked. "My seventeen year old could really use some help."

"In fact, I do," I replied. "And I happen to have an opening next week."

"Sorry I'm late," I said, sliding into the booth where Tano sat, glass of red wine in hand.

It was early evening and I had just seen my first client that afternoon. Tano and I had a date for *apero* afterwards – just the two of us – outside of Makena's crèche. The doors did not open until 6:00, and we had gotten into the habit of meeting at 5:30 for a drink before picking up our daughter and going home together.

This small bistro, with its deep ochre walls and old wooden tables had become the backdrop against which we had been rebuilding our...*what?* I didn't yet dare say marriage. There were still too many open wounds.

Shortly after being reunited with Tano, I had revealed my affair with Jacques. He was as angry and hurt as I had been when I'd discovered his relationship with Estelle.

But in some ways, it was our respective love affairs that rekindled our own.

Bouts of fighting – *how <u>could</u> you?* – and the tearful apologies and explanations that invariably followed led us back to the tenderness and ardor that reminded us of *us* – of who we had been as a couple before the stress of our life in East Africa had kicked in.

Ultimately, we had to retire our individual humiliations and live up to the fact that we had done the same thing to each other, motivated by frustration and loneliness. And though the healing process was slow – learning to trust again is hard work - we agreed early on that the best redemption would be learning from our mistakes and saving our family.

These meetings at this cozy bistro were part of the comfortable détente into which we'd settled while we waited for time to take the edge off of some of the pain.

In the meantime we had plenty of other matters to discuss, born from the major lesson our years in East Africa had taught us: that for us to have a satisfying marriage, we *both* had to be able to fulfill our dreams.

"So how did it go?" Tano asked, brushing my lips lightly with his.

"It was great."

I poured out the details of my first session with the seventeen year old. She had arrived fifteen minutes late, reeking of cigarettes and opposition, too much blue eye shadow contrasting with too-skimpy clothes.

"I hate life," she snarled, plopping back against the burgundy velvet. "But cool chairs."

At the end of the session she asked if she could come back the following week. "Can I give your number to my friend? She needs a psychiatrist, too."

Apparently Shirley was not the only one to make this mistake.

Tano laughed when I recounted this story.

I laughed too.

We leaned on each other.

EPILOGUE: PARIS, 2011

It is a warm evening in late May. I am hurrying to lock up my office – an intimate space practically at the foot of the Eiffel Tower – so I can meet up with Makena, now eleven. She and I will go together to pick up her little brother, my son, who is five years old, from school. We still live in our cozy apartment in the 11th *arrondissement*, but I stopped working out of the living room when my practice became too busy to manage -- and we had a new baby boy in the house.

The presentation I gave to the International Women's Club was picked up by other expatriate organizations, and within a year I was regularly giving talks to different women's clubs, embassies, and international schools on a variety of topics ranging from cultural adjustment and international mobility to dealing with depression, anxiety and substance abuse. The connections I made as a consultant fed my private practice and eventually landed me a contract with an international university in Paris, providing the counseling services to their student body.

Fortunately, the Epicentre office is in our neighborhood, which makes it easy for Tano to accompany and pick up our kids from school. When he's not traveling, that is. Since we settled in Paris, he has continued to spend about 30% of his time in the field. Among others, there have been more ebola and cholera epidemics, measles outbreaks, malaria and of course, the multicentric clinical trial that he started in 2001, testing drug combinations to find a new treatment protocol for sleeping sickness.

For the ten years we have been living in Paris, Tano has been going back and forth between the Democratic Republic of Congo, Congo-Brazzaville, and Uganda as the principal investigator of a study that tested a combination of the old sleeping sickness drug – eflornithine - and nifurtimox, a drug used to treat Chagas Disease, endemic in Argentina and other parts of Latin America. The NECT trial (Nifurtimox-Eflornithine Combination Therapy) was conducted in areas so remote, that the voyage to some of the study sites took three days and involved multiple airplanes, motorcycles, and pirogues down the Congo River.

In late 2008, Tano finalized the data analysis and Epicentre presented the results to the scientific community. In May, 2009, the World Health Organization voted to include the new treatment protocol on its list of Essential Medicines. This was a huge triumph for Tano, Epicentre and MSF, and most importantly, for those thousands of Africans with sleeping sickness, for whom the treatment will literally mean life instead of death.

Tano and Jacques have continued to work together, although they are no longer friends. Jacques and I have never seen each other again. Sometimes I wonder if he ever thinks about me, but I don't really need to know. And as far as Estelle is concerned, Tano told me he broke all contact with her when I left him. A few times over these years I've asked if he's heard from her, but a while back I stopped even wondering.

Having stretched our marriage as far as we did - having tested it, neglected it, turned our backs on it entirely – and finally, having *chosen* it, I don't really worry about affairs anymore. I know Tano loves me. I know he adores our kids. And I know that life with an MSF cowboy won't ever be dull.

What I know about myself is that, if I had to do it all over again, I would still choose the tumult, for it was there that I found confidence and inspiration.

In the end, we both got what we wanted. Tano got his career in humanitarian medicine *and* a wife and children – not the most evident balance for an MSF cowboy.

And me?

I learned to be the leader of my own life, and in that, taught a cowboy how to trail sometimes, too.

I got two awesome kids who, although not purebred Parisian, have the sense of belonging that evaded me when I was young.

And I got *my* career, a bustling, active counseling and consultancy practice in which I see teenagers and adults with a wide range of problems.

But I will always feel a particular bond with the many trailing spouses who come through my office, depressed and hopeless that they will ever land on their feet.

I ask these women the important questions I asked myself those years I spent in East Africa. *What do you want from your life? Are your expectations realistic? Do you feel supported? Do you feel safe?*

The most valuable work happens when we get to the questions that I struggled with for so long — questions that cut to the core of one's identity.

What gives your life a sense of meaning? What is your purpose?

It occurs to me every year when the anniversary of our rupture comes around that I had once doubted that Tano and I could ever be happy together again. And frequently, as I look out the window to the wonderful rooftops of Paris, I remember what it was like to feel so lost and destabilized, and I'm filled with relief to have reached safety and fulfillment.

I look out the window and I know I am home.

NOTE TO THE READER AND ACKNOWLEDGEMENTS

Trailing is a memoir based on some of the experiences I lived over four and a half years in East Africa as the wife of a Médecins Sans Frontières doctor.

There are several reasons I wrote this book.

The first is because I wanted to recount what it was like for me, a young wife and budding professional, to accompany my husband on *his* career path, putting my own aspirations into question. That there are thousands of "trailing spouses" in the world today, and that there are so many implications associated with "trailing," makes this phenomenon an important one to describe. While every story is unique, many of the issues I struggled with – identity loss, not knowing how to fit in or craft a new life, resentment towards my husband – are "universals" for many accompanying spouses.

The second motivation I had in writing *Trailing* was to describe the public health crises, and the suffering and injustice that the work of MSF opened my eyes to. Even if I was sometimes at odds with the MSF team, feeling like a fish out of water in their presence, I feel deeply privileged to have lived in such proximity to them over those years. Before going on mission with my husband, I had no idea what it meant to give one's life for a conviction; no idea what it meant to work tirelessly round the clock to assuage suffering – and sometimes to no avail.

Lastly, I wanted to describe trauma, anxiety, and depression in accessible terms – and hopefully illustrate the impact these mental conditions can have on quality of life and in turn, interpersonal relationships. What I lived through in Kenya is anecdotal evidence that victims – and witnesses - of violence need to receive some type of debriefing, to process what happened and to hopefully minimize post traumatic stress.

I emphasize that *Trailing* is <u>based on some</u> of the experiences I lived in the years we spent in Kenya and Uganda, because those years included such a rapid passage of events it was impossible for me to tell a coherent story that included everything and everyone who was present at that time. For this reason, many of the characters in *Trailing* are composites, people that I created from the real ones I interacted with. Also, in describing the issues and epidemics that MSF was dealing with, as well as the situations my own work confronted me with, I condensed, blended or modified some circumstances, for the sake of protecting identity or improving narrative flow.

Regarding health statistics or money expenditure, I did not consistently verify exact dates and numbers. For me it was more important to describe impressions, such as those of desperation and hopelessness, or the waste of money, than to delineate exactly how many people were sick, or how much money was spent. If anything, I have understated the poverty and illness in zones where people do not have access to medicine and healthcare, as well as the enormous gap between rich and poor.

Finally, I am aware that as a practicing psychotherapist I am taking a risk by exposing this private side of my life. I thought about justifying this by explaining that the events of *Trailing* seem like another lifetime, and that the young woman narrating the story is someone I no longer know. This is all true. But the real reason I am compelled to tell my story is because of the way the personal and the professional are ultimately woven together. A therapist is, before anything else, just another human being, with his or her unique history. My firsthand understanding of some of the issues described in this book, such as trauma, depression, anxiety, and relational struggles informs the work I do with clients today.

Special acknowledgement goes to the family of Cecie Goetz, the young woman who was murdered in Uganda. I was so influenced by her story that it was important for me to include it with my own.

I also want to acknowledge my dear friend and mentor Dominic Cappello for showing me how to make things happen. This book would never have been written if he hadn't convinced me that I, too, could write a book…and that I had a story worth telling.

Special thanks also go to John Baxter, narrative therapist extraordinaire. Our work together will always stay with me.

The biggest acknowledgement of all goes to my husband, Tano, a real cowboy, steadfast and strong. One of the most important exercises in writing, and then rewriting, and then rewriting *again* the text of this narrative, was the act of letting go of blame, and learning to take responsibility for *my* part – good and bad – in our life together those early years of our marriage.

SOURCES

Paéz, Fito. Y Dale Alegria A Mi Corazon. Tercer Mundo. WEA Corp, 1990

Alpha Blondy. "Masada." Masada. Blue Note Records, 1992

Russell, Leon. "This Masquerade." Lyrics performed by George Benson. Breezin'. Warner Brothers, 1976

Perry, Joe and Tyler, Steven. "F.I.N.E." Pump. Geffen, 1989

Printed in Great Britain
by Amazon.co.uk, Ltd.,
Marston Gate.